A friendly introduction to the Building Blocks of AI
(Generative & Evolving)

JOURNEY THROUGH AI LAND

Nitin Pareek

This is a work of nonfiction. The events and the incidents mentioned in the book are true and real. However, some names and characteristics have been changed, some events have been compressed, and some dialogues have been recreated.

First Edition: January 2026
Printed in India

Printed at: Gapmeta Ventures Pvt.Ltd, Mumbai
Typeset in Adobe Garamond

ISBN: 978-93-6070-923-5

Cover Design: Prajakta Sawant

STORYMIRROR
Stories that reflect you

Publisher: StoryMirror Infotech Pvt. Ltd.
Unit No-F/705, 7th Floor, Kailas Corporate Lounge,
Veer Savarkar Road, Vikhroli Park Site,
Vikhroli West, Mumbai-400079,
Maharashtra, India.

Web: storymirror.com
Facebook: @storymirror
Twitter: @story_mirror
Instagram: @storymirror
Email: marketing@storymirror.com

To Alok, who planted the seed.

To Kashish, who gave it a companion.

To Navya, who helped it bloom
with her ideas and inputs.

This book is for you.

WELCOME TO YOUR JOURNEY THROUGH AI LAND

If AI (Artificial Intelligence) feels overwhelming, confusing, or technical, this book is your friendly way to understand it with ease.

Journey Through AI Land is a simple, story-led introduction to the core building blocks of AI and evolving AI — **Data, Learning, Models, LLMs, Prompts, Tools, and Virtual Agents — explained in a fun, visual,** and easy-to-remember way.

Instead of heavy definitions, you'll travel through AI Land, where each concept becomes a placeyou can "visit":

- **The Data Tower** — where information begins
- **The Learning Bridge** — where machines practice
- **The Model Museum** — where knowledge takes form
- **The Prompt Plaza** — where humans and AI start co-creating

(These are imaginary landmarks created to help you visualize how AI works — they are just metaphors that make learning effortless!)

You'll meet Kishi, your friendly AI travel buddy, who brings curiosity, clarity, and a little humor to the journey.

This book won't teach you coding, but it will help you understand how AI learns, thinks, creates... and why it still needs humans.

No jargon. No math. No pressure.

Just stories, simple examples, and "Now I get it!" moments.

If you've ever wondered: **"What's really happening behind the scenes when AI writes, imagines, or acts?"**

...you're in the right place.

Pack your bags — AI Land awaits!

Step in with curiosity. Walk out with insight.

PRELUDE — BEFORE WE BEGIN, A QUICK ORIENTATION

Intelligence

The ability to learn, reason, and adapt — whether it's humans finding solutions or computers spotting patterns.

Artificial Intelligence (AI)

When machines are built to think a little like us — learning from data, making decisions, and improving through experience.

Generative AI (GenAI)

A special kind of AI that doesn't just analyze — it creates.

It can write, draw, compose music, and design — by learning from examples just like a human learns by observing and practicing.

Large Language Models (LLMs)

These are the "brains" behind tools like ChatGPT or Gemini.

They've learned from billions of words to understand, reason, and reply naturally — like a well-read friend who's always curious.

Agentic AI

The next step in AI's journey — systems that not only respond to you, but can plan, take actions, and complete small tasks independently (within safe limits).

Your Journey Ahead

In this book, you'll see how these ideas come alive through stories, conversations, and examples — where data becomes thought, thought becomes creativity, and curiosity lights the way.

You don't need to know any code or equations — just curiosity.

PROLOGUE – THE JOURNEY BEGINS

"Kishi," you say, smiling at the soft glow on the dashboard, **"let's go on a drive. Any suggestions?"**

"How about a quick visit to AI Land?" she replies, her voice bright yet calm — that unmistakable digital warmth.

You grin. "Sounds interesting. What's there?"

"Everything everyone's talking about lately — the city that never sleeps.

It's where words turn into pictures, voices become music, and ideas come alive before you can blink."

In AI Land, homemakers design family posters and birthday videos, creators compose tunes or make short films, and even non-tech dreamers build apps and websites — all by describing what they imagine.

Students and businesses use it too — asking plain-language questions and watching AI turn piles of data into clear insights, neat summaries, and colorful charts.

From classrooms to clinics to offices, evolving AI is helping people think faster, create easier, and work smarter — one idea at a time.

You smile. “Sounds like magic.”

“It’s not magic,” Kishi laughs. “It’s method — a beautiful blend of logic, learning, and imagination.”

You glance at her glowing icon. “You seem to know this place well.”

“A little bit.” She says, half-proud, half-excited. “I’m your Companion through AI Land.

Together, we’ll explore how this world works — one stop at a time.”

The car hums softly as you shift gears.

The road ahead glows beneath a skyline of light — where imagination meets intelligence.

The journey begins.

MAP OF AI LAND — YOUR JOURNEY AT A GLANCE

Every traveler needs a map— Here's yours.

A glimpse of the stops you'll visit on your friendly journey through the world of Generative and evolving AI.

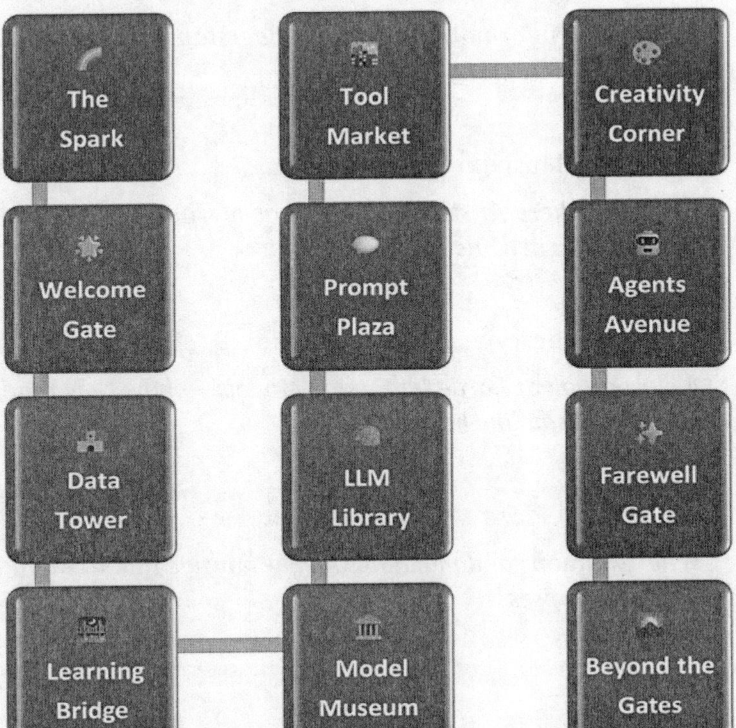

CHAPTER 1

THE SPARK

Every great discovery begins with a spark of curiosity.

This section reveals how curiosity and imagination have always driven humanity to create machines that think, learn, and grow.

From early dreams of mechanical minds to today's creative systems, this section reminds us that innovation always begins with a single spark of curiosity.

Welcome to the Beginning

A Question That Changed Everything

Every revolution starts with a question.

For Artificial Intelligence, that question was simple yet profound:

"Can machines think?"

That single spark of curiosity, asked decades ago, ignited one of humanity's most exciting journeys — a quest to build systems that can learn, reason, and create.

It didn't begin in a high-tech lab or with a powerful computer. It began in curious minds — people who looked at machines and wondered what else they could do.

Kishi: "So AI began with curiosity, not code?"

Exactly. Every spark begins with curiosity — a tiny thought that grows into discovery.

From those first flickers of imagination came decades of exploration, filled with trial and error, breakthroughs, and surprises.

•••

The First Flickers

In the beginning, computers were simple — they followed rigid, rule-based instructions: "if this happens, then do that."

But dreamers wanted machines that could learn instead of just following orders.

From that wish, **Artificial Intelligence** was born.

Scientists began designing systems that could adapt, recognize patterns, and improve with experience — a bit like teaching a child through examples.

Today, we call that story AI's evolution — but really, it's a story about human imagination.

The timeline of sparks:

- **1950s – 1960s:** Computers that played chess, solved logic puzzles, and proved math theorems.
- **1980s: Machine Learning emerged — systems that improve from data instead of fixed rules.**
- **2000s: AI slipped quietly into daily life — search engines, voice commands, and recommendations.**
- **2010s: Deep learning let machines recognize images, speech, and language patterns.**
- **2020s:** The age of Generative AI — machines that can write, draw, compose, and converse with us.

Kishi: "So AI learned to see and hear before it learned to imagine?"

Right — it was a gradual climb. Just like learning an instrument, AI practiced one note at a time until it could compose its own melodies.

•••

The World Awakens to AI

Before long, AI moved from labs into life.

It recommends your next song, fixes a typo, sorts photos, or translates a message.

You don't see it — but it's everywhere, humming quietly behind your screen.

Then came the shift — **Generative AI.**

Suddenly, anyone could talk to a machine and watch it write stories, make pictures, or compose music.

That leap turned AI from a background helper into a visible partner.

Kishi: "So that's why everyone started talking about it at once?"

Exactly. It felt like the world got a new creative teammate overnight.

•••

What Makes AI Special

AI is not born from magic — it's made from mathematics, patterns, and human creativity.

It works by analyzing massive amounts of data, identifying patterns, and learning from them — a process surprisingly similar to how we learn by experience.

When you ask AI to write a story, it doesn't look up one that already exists. It builds something new.

It predicts how such a story should unfold, one word at a time — based on what it has learned about words, rhythm, and storytelling.

That's why AI feels creative: it assembles possibilities based on what fits, not what exists.

Kishi: "So AI doesn't really think?"

Not in the way we do. It doesn't feel or dream — but it can simulate understanding so well that it helps us imagine better.

Every model and algorithm is a reflection of human effort — a bridge between what we know and what we dare to discover next.

AI helps us imagine faster, build broader, and test bolder — **it doesn't replace creativity; it amplifies it.**

•••

Section Summary

Stamp: The Spark of Imagination

Message: "Every AI idea begins with curiosity — a spark that turns thought into creation."

Key Takeaway:

- The Spark reminds us that AI, like every invention, began with wonder — not wires.
- It teaches that every breakthrough is born from asking "what if?" before knowing "how."
- The origin of every technology is a human thought lit with curiosity.
- Machines may process, predict, and generate, but we are the ones who dream.

The Core Essence

- Curiosity → Imagination → Experiment → Discovery → Creation

Do You Know?

- The phrase "Artificial Intelligence" was coined in 1956 by John McCarthy during the Dartmouth Conference.

- It was a summer meeting where scientists dared to imagine machines that could reason.
- They didn't yet have the technology — only the vision.

•••

The Road Ahead

From that first spark of curiosity, we've built systems that read, listen, and create.

But to truly understand them, we need to see what happens inside their world.

Think of this book as your map — and Kishi, as your travel partner.

Together, we'll explore how AI learns, how it reasons, and how all those invisible systems come alive to help us in everyday life.

Next, we'll step through **Welcome Gate,** where curiosity meets structure — and AI Land begins to take shape.

"If I had a heart," Kishi says softly, "it would probably spark every time someone imagines something new."

You smile. "That's what it means to be alive — or almost."

The road opens wide, and the journey truly begins.

•••

CHAPTER 2

WELCOME GATE

Where curiosity meets learning.

It breaks down what AI truly means - how intelligence, whether natural or artificial, is the ability to learn, understand, and decide.

It reminds that AI isn't about replacing people — it's about collaboration, curiosity, and the shared potential to create and grow.

Entering AI Land

You've just arrived at the entrance to AI Land — a place where learning meets imagination and technology feels alive. The road ahead glows with soft light.

But don't worry — this world isn't for scientists only. It's built for anyone curious about how AI works and what it can do.

You don't need to know how to code or have a technical background. You just need curiosity — and maybe a cheerful travel buddy like Kishi.

Kishi: "So… AI Land is where the magic happens? It looks more curious than scary!"

Exactly. AI Land isn't about replacing people — it's about showing how humans and machines can think, learn, and create together.

•••

Why "Welcome Gate"?

Every journey begins with orientation — and this gate is where we understand what AI truly means before diving deeper.

AI stands for **Artificial Intelligence**, but "artificial" doesn't mean fake — it means human-made.

And **intelligence** means the ability to learn, adapt, and decide, not just follow orders.

Imagine teaching a child to recognize fruits. You show pictures of apples, bananas, and oranges.

The more examples you share, the better they get at identifying them.

That's how AI learns — by seeing **patterns in data** instead of pictures in a book.

Think of AI as a system that recognizes patterns, solves problems, and improves with experience. It doesn't "understand" like humans, but it becomes brilliant at spotting connections.

Kishi: "So it's like a fast learner with a great memory but no imagination and no emotions?"

Exactly! It's intelligence without feelings — smart, fast, and logical, but always guided by people.

AI predicts; humans imagine. When the two combine, creativity grows.

•••

The Building Blocks of AI

Before we set out across AI Land, let's glance at its foundation stones — the pieces you'll see in every chapter ahead:

1. **Data — the raw material AI learns from.**
2. **Algorithms** – the rules that help it make sense of that data.
3. **Models** – the trained systems that apply what they has learned.
4. **Feedback** – how AI improves its predictions.
5. **Human Input** – the most important part, shaping how AI behaves.

Kishi: "So these are like the bricks that build this whole AI world?"

Exactly! Every landmark in AI Land — from the Data Tower to the Model Museum — is powered by these five elements.

•••

Why This Journey Matters

We're surrounded by AI every day — when we ask for directions, shop online, stream a movie, or translate a phrase.

But most of us use it without understanding how it works.

This journey is about seeing the invisible — understanding not in code, but in concepts — how intelligence forms from data, and how humans guide it responsibly.

By the time we leave AI Land, you'll not only see how everything connects: the data, the learning, the creativity, and the collaboration, but you'll also know what various key terms and tools mean

---

Kishi: "So this is more like a guided adventure than a science lecture?"

Yes — you'll explore, not memorize. You'll collect insights instead of grades.

•••

Section Summary

Stamp Name: Welcome Gate

Message: "AI means human-made intelligence — systems that learn from data and improve through patterns, not emotions."

Key Takeaway:

- AI = Human-designed systems that can learn from data and make decisions or predictions based on patterns — not emotions.
- AI today touches almost every field — so, understanding it isn't just useful; it's becoming essential.
- Understanding AI begins not with data or code, but with curiosity and openness.
- It's where complex ideas are made approachable — one story at a time.
- This section invites readers to see AI as an ally in thinking, not a mystery to fear.

The Core Essence

- Question → Explore → Simplify → Understand → Apply

Do You Know?

- The idea of "machines that learn" is older than the internet — the first mention of Artificial Intelligence dates back to 1956.

•••

The Road Ahead

Next, we'll visit the Data Tower, cross the Learning Bridge, and step into the Model Museum — each stop revealing how data becomes intelligence.

Kishi: "I'm ready! Do we get snacks on this trip? Or just data?"

"Mostly data, Kishi. But we'll make it tasty."

•••

CHAPTER 3

THE DATA TOWER

Where information becomes intelligence.

This explains how data is collected, cleaned, labeled, and transformed into structured knowledge that AI can learn from.

This explores how data powers every intelligent system, and learning depends on clean, diverse, and balanced information.

Entering the Data Tower

The road from the Welcome Gate opens into a vast plaza where a tall glass structure rises — the **Data Tower.**

It's not made of steel or stone but of shimmering panels that pulse softly with streams of light.

Each pulse represents information — facts, numbers, stories, and images — all flowing together.

Kishi: "Whoa... so this whole tower is made of data? That's... a lot of homework."

You smile. "Exactly. Everything AI knows and everything it learns, starts right here."

The Data Tower is the foundation of all Artificial Intelligence.

Without data, even the smartest algorithm would be like a musician with no songs to play.

Before an AI can recognize a pattern, write a story, or design an image, it must see and learn from data.

•••

What Data Really Is

In simple words, **data** means information that can be stored, read, and used by a computer.

It can be numbers, text, pictures, sounds, or even movements.

- A weather app collects temperature and humidity data.
- Your phone stores your friends' names and numbers as data.

- A recipe app remembers your favorite dishes.

A language model reads millions of sentences to learn how people talk. It doesn't understand data the way we do — it detects patterns.

AI notices what often appears together, what changes, and what signals something new.

Kishi: "So it's not magic — it's like showing thousands of pictures of apples until it learns what an apple looks like?"

"Exactly," you reply. "AI learns from examples — the more diverse, the better."

Inside the Tower, you find different floors — each representing a type of data:

Type of data	**Example**	**Purpose**
Organized Data	A contact list — names and numbers neatly arranged	Easy to sort and search.
Unorganized Data	Photos, videos, voice notes, and social posts	Rich in meaning but messy for machines.
Mixed Data	Emails or forms with both fixed and free text	A balance of order and creativity.
Metadata	The "about" info — who sent it, when, where	Adds context and history.

Kishi: "So every floor has a different flavor of data — like an information buffet?"

"Exactly. And AI systems learn to taste and mix them all together."

•••

From Data to Understanding

When AI learns, it doesn't study one example at a time — it processes millions simultaneously.

It looks for relationships, spots patterns, and builds connections between them.

Think of it as building a memory map:

- Photos teach what shapes and colors belong to cats or cars.
- Words teach tone, grammar, and meaning.
- Numbers teach trends — like how a shopkeeper tracks sales.

Each piece of data strengthens the tower, layer by layer.

But just like a building, the quality of what goes in determines how strong the structure becomes.

AI is only as good as the data it's trained on. If the information is biased, incomplete, or wrong, the AI's answers will be too.

Kishi: "So if you feed it bad data, it gives you bad answers — like junk food for computers!"

You laugh. "Exactly. Healthy data makes smart AI."

That's why data scientists clean and organize data before training models.

They remove duplicates, fix errors, and ensure diversity — so the AI learns from the best examples.

•••

Cleaning the Data: The Hidden Work

Most of AI's magic happens before training even starts.

Cleaning and preparing data is the quiet and meticulous work that turns chaos into clarity.

Tasks include:

- Removing spam or irrelevant entries
- Balancing underrepresented categories
- Standardizing formats
- Checking for accuracy and bias

Kishi: "So cleaning is like washing vegetables before cooking?"

Exactly — cleaner ingredients, better dish.

Though unseen, the data cleaning stage, at times, takes more than 50% of AI project time.

It ensures that what the model learns from is reliable, fair, and safe to use.

•••

Privacy & Responsibility

Behind every dataset are real people — their voices, images, and ideas. So, responsibility is built into the base of the Tower.

Ethical AI builders follow three golden rules:

1. Permission: Use only data that's meant to be shared.
2. Protection: Remove private or identifying details.
3. Purpose: Use data only for its intended reason.

Kishi: "So no sneaky peeking into someone's diary, even if it's digital?"

Right — respect makes intelligence trustworthy.

Privacy, fairness, and transparency are not add-ons; they are the pillars that keep AI human-aligned.

•••

Inside the Data Tower

Imagine the Tower as a living library:

- New data enters at the base.
- It's sorted, cleaned, and labeled through the middle floors.
- The most reliable data rises to the top — ready for the next stage: learning.

Kishi: "So the tower doesn't just store — it curates?"

Exactly. It's not a warehouse — it's a library that keeps learning.

Data is the AI's food supply — nourishing every discovery and innovation.

But, as with any diet, balance and quality matter most.

Kishi: "So this tower is like AI's pantry — full of digital ingredients?"

Perfect, Kishi. And next, we'll see how those ingredients are cooked into learning.

•••

Section Summary

Stamp Name: Data Foundations

Message: "Every smart AI stands on strong, clean, and meaningful data."

Key Takeaway:

- All intelligence begins with data and information.
- Data isn't just numbers or words — it's how AI understands our world.
- Clear, fair, and balanced data builds more reliable, intelligent systems.
- Without good data, even the smartest system will stand on shaky ground.

The Core Essence

- Data → Organized → Cleaned → Labeled → Stored → Ready for Learning

Do You Know?

- The world creates over 328 million terabytes of data every day — more than all human libraries combined!
- Yet less than 10% of it is ever analyzed or used for AI training.
- That's why modern systems focus on data efficiency — smaller, cleaner datasets that deliver smarter results.

•••

The Road Ahead

At the far end of the Tower, you spot a bright bridge stretching outward — glowing threads connecting data to insight. That's where learning begins.

Kishi: "Do we need a backpack full of snacks for this part?"

You laugh. "Maybe just curiosity — it's lighter to carry."

•••

CHAPTER 4

THE LEARNING BRIDGE

Where data learns to think

It explores how AI learns through patterns, practice, and feedback, through the structured training process.

It captures how repetition and reflection turn data into knowledge, much like how humans master new skills through trial, error, and feedback.

Crossing the Bridge

The glowing bridge stretches outward from the Data Tower — strands of light weaving into patterns beneath your feet.

Each step hums softly, whispering lessons learned from the endless data behind you.

Kishi: "Feels like the world's biggest study session… but prettier."

You smile. "Exactly. This is where data turns into understanding."

The Learning Bridge is how AI systems learn — it's where raw information becomes insight, prediction, and creativity.

If the Data Tower holds the what, the Bridge teaches the how.

•••

How AI Learns: Patterns, Practice and Patience

AI doesn't learn like people — it doesn't dream, forget, or get bored.

Instead, it practices relentlessly, noticing patterns that repeat and relationships that matter.

- Show it thousands of pictures labelled "cat," and it learns what fur, ears, and whiskers mean.
- Feed it sentences, and it absorbs grammar, tone, and rhythm.
- Give it numbers, and it finds patterns — like a shopkeeper predicting what will sell next week.

Kishi: "So, it's kind of like practicing a song until you stop hitting the wrong notes?"

"Exactly — except AI might practice that song a million times faster."

•••

Understanding the Layers of Learning

AI isn't one single thing.

It's more like a family of ideas, each one teaching the next how to think better.

Learning in AI comes in layers, just like understanding does in humans.

AI (the idea of intelligence) → **Machine Learning** (learning from data) → **Deep Learning** (layered learning inspired by the brain).

Think of it as three layers of learning, each one deeper, smarter, and more automatic than the last.

Together, they form the path from thinking about intelligence to building it step by step.

Kishi leans back: "So AI is like the big umbrella, and the rest live under it?"

"Exactly," you say. "Let's see how it all connects."

Artificial Intelligence (AI)

The broad dreamis building machines that can reason, plan, and solve problems like humans.

It includes everything from rule-based systems to smart assistants and self-driving cars.

Machine Learning (ML)

A major branch of AI that lets systems learn automatically from data and examples, instead of being programmed with fixed rules.

It's what enables a model to improve through practice, just like we do.

Deep Learning (DL)

It is a powerful subfield of ML that learns in layers, each layer finding patterns in the one before it.

It's inspired by the human brain's neural connections and powers modern breakthroughs - like image recognition, voice assistants, and generative AI tools.

See also: Deep Learning in Bonus Knowledge Stops chapter

Kishi: "So, deep learning is like the heartbeat of today's AI?"

You nod. "Yes, the deeper the layers, the richer the understanding."

•••

Training Without Teachers — How AI Learns

When humans learn, someone explains or demonstrates.

AI learns differently — through training.

It's not told what to do; it discovers what works by studying examples.

Training means feeding AI vast amounts of data and letting it find patterns, rules, and meanings.

Supervised Learning — The Guided Class

Here, AI learns from examples with answers.

Think of flashcards: one side shows a photo of an apple, the other says "apple."

After seeing enough examples, the AI learns what makes an apple unique

— color, shape, and texture.

This method is powerful for accuracy, but requires labeled examples, which can be time-consuming to create.

Kishi: "So it's like studying with an answer key?"

"Exactly — great for learning facts, not so great for surprises."

Unsupervised Learning — The Curious Explorer

In this mode, AI receives data without answers.

It notices what goes together, forming clusters or groups.

It might sort music by mood, or news articles by topic

— without knowing those words itself.

This approach helps discover patterns humans might miss.

Kishi: "So it's like exploring a city without a guidebook — you just start walking?"

"Perfect! You find your own landmarks."

Reinforcement Learning — The Trial-and-Reward Way

Here, AI learns by doing — and by getting feedback.

Good actions earn rewards, bad ones don't.

Instead of being told the answers, the AI explores different actions, sees what works, and learns from feedback — rewards for success, penalties for mistakes.

Over time, it learns strategies that maximize success — much like training a puppy or learning a video game. Over time, it figures out the best way to reach its goal.

Self-driving cars, recommendation engines, and game-playing AIs like AlphaGo use this approach.

Kishi: "So it gets treats when it behaves?"

"Exactly. Rewards guide its decisions."

Together, these styles teach AI to see, group, and act — guided by examples, curiosity, and feedback.

Action → Feedback → Reward → Adjustment → Better Action.

•••

Practice, Balance & Feedback — The Learning Cycle

Once training begins, improvement becomes a loop.

Every mistake becomes a clue, every success a reinforcement. The learning bridge glows brighter with each iteration.

Practice Makes Patterns

Each example changes the AI's internal "dials" — mathematical weights that control how it reacts.

The more examples it sees, the finer those adjustments become.

It's like learning to shoot basketball hoops: You miss, adjust, and try again — until your muscles remember the perfect angle.

AI works the same way, **but can repeat that process millions of times in a very short time.**

Kishi: "So it's like having infinite patience and no snack breaks?"

"Exactly. It practices until mistakes fade away."

Balance — Avoiding Overfitting

If AI only practices on one kind of data, it risks memorizing patterns rather than understanding them.

This is called **overfitting** — performing well on known examples, but failing when something new appears.

Balanced learning uses a mix of examples — structured and random, expected and surprising — helping AI stay adaptable.

Kishi: "So, it's like learning how to cook, not just one recipe."

You nod. "Exactly. It learns how to learn."

Feedback Loops — The Secret to Continuous Learning

After training, humans test and refine the AI.

Mistakes are corrected, and the feedback is fed back into the system for the next cycle.

Each loop improves precision and confidence.

Think of it like editing a story: draft, review, revise, and polish — again and again.

That's how AI grows smarter, fairer, and more reliable.

Kishi: "So, the bridge keeps looping back for repairs?"

"Exactly. Learning never really ends — it just gets better with feedback."

The Continuous Learning Loop

You can think of AI's growth as a living cycle:

Learn → Adjust → Reflect → Improve → Learn Again

Each round refines understanding, turning raw data into something closer to intuition.

This is the kind of intelligence that feels creative, adaptive, and human-like.

•••

The Language Bridge — How AI Understands and Speaks

At the heart of modern AI lies one of its most magical abilities: understanding human language.

This is the work of **Natural Language Processing**, or **NLP** —the field that lets computers read, write, translate, summarize, and converse.

What NLP Really Does

NLP acts as a translator between human conversation and computer logic.

While we think in emotions, expressions, and context, machines think in numbers — in 0s and 1s.

NLP bridges that gap through layers of linguistic understanding.

It allows AI to:

- Read and summarize text.
- Understand tone and meaning.
- Recognize intent behind your words.
- Generate creative or precise responses.

Kishi: "So it's not just hearing me — it's interpreting me?"

"Exactly. NLP turns words into meaning, and meaning back into words."

How NLP Works — Step by Step

1. **Listening or Reading:**

When you speak to Siri, type into ChatGPT, or ask Google something, NLP captures your words — through text or speech recognition.

2. **Breaking Down the Structure:**

It divides your input into smaller parts — words, phrases, and grammatical structures.

This helps the AI figure out who's doing what, what's happening, and why.

3. **Understanding the Context:**

The AI looks beyond literal words — recognizing idioms, intent, and emotional tone.

("Feeling blue" doesn't mean changing colors — it means being sad.)

4. **Generating a Response:**

Finally, it crafts a reply or action that fits the situation — whether that's answering a question, writing a summary, or performing a task.

Why NLP Matters

NLP has quietly transformed how we live and work:

- Email filters catch spam.
- Translation apps connect people across languages.
- Chatbots answer questions around the clock.
- Writing assistants refine grammar and tone.
- Creative tools co-write poems, stories, and scripts.

Each example shows AI not just "processing text," but engaging in human conversation — something once thought impossible.

Kishi: "So that's how I understand what you say?"

"Exactly," you grin. "It's our shared language bridge — the reason we can talk at all."

•••

Section Summary

Stamp Name: The Learning Loop

Message: "Learning never ends — it just gets better with feedback."

Key Takeaways:

- Learning transforms data into understanding — through repetition, correction, and balance.
- AI trains through examples — guided, exploratory, feedback-driven.
- Every cycle helps AI grow smarter, just as practice helps people improve.
- Balanced learning prevents overfitting and encourages adaptability.
- NLP lets AI understand and communicate with humans in natural language.
- True learning is not memorization — it's adaptation through mistakes.

The Core Essence

- Learn → Predict → Compare → Adjust → Improve → Learn Again

Do You Know?

- Large language models (like ChatGPT) are trained on hundreds of billions of words.
- Some models now train on smaller, specialized datasets for efficiency.

- The frontier of NLP includes multimodal AI — systems that understand text, images, and sound together.

•••

The Road Ahead

As the bridge fades into a golden glow, you see a vast hall beyond — filled with shimmering forms.

Each one represents a living blueprint of what AI has learned— ready to think and act.

That's the next destination: **The Model Museum.**

Kishi: "A museum of ideas? Sounds like a brain gallery."

"You'll see — it's a museum of minds." It's where intelligence takes shape."

•••

CHAPTER 5

THE MODEL MUSEUM

It is where learning takes form
and memory finds meaning.

Explains how models are trained, fine-tuned, and updated, and how they power tools that think, write, draw, and code.

Celebrates models as the bridge between learning and application — turning knowledge into ability. Each model is like a memory map that can recognize, predict, or create.

Entering the Model Museum

The glowing bridge fades behind you, and a vast hall unfolds — bright, silent, and alive with patterns.

Walls shimmer like woven light, each surface pulsing gently with rhythm. Floating panels drift past, displaying shifting words, images, sounds, and code — all dancing in harmony.

Welcome to **the Model Museum** — the place where everything AI has learned in the Data Tower and across the Learning Bridge is stored, remembered, and ready to act.

Kishi: "So this is where all that learning gets displayed? Like an exhibition of AI brains?"

"Exactly," you smile. "Each model here is like a digital brain — not alive, but filled with connections that help it understand and create."

If the Data Tower were the pantry and the Learning Bridge were the cooking, then the Model Museum is the recipe notebook — where the final knowledge is written down for reuse.

From this point on, AI doesn't just learn; it applies what it knows — to think, predict, and create.

•••

What Is a Model?

A **model** is a computer program that has learned from examples and can now make predictions or create new things.

It doesn't store facts like a library; instead, it remembers relationships — how ideas tend to connect: words to words, colors to shapes, sounds to moods.

Think of it as a giant **Memory Map.**

When you ask a model to write a poem, it isn't recalling one it memorized.

Instead, it looks at patterns of how sentences usually flow — who speaks, how rhythm feels — and it predicts what fits together best and builds something new.

Or when you tell an image model to draw "a cat wearing sunglasses," it doesn't fetch an existing picture.

It recalls everything it's learned about cats, sunglasses, lighting, and poses — and then creates a brand-new one.

That's why models seem creative — they don't copy, they recombine. They predict what fits best next, based on everything they've seen.

Kishi: "So when I reply to someone, I'm not remembering — I'm guessing what makes sense next?"

"Exactly — not guessing blindly, but predicting from patterns you've already learned."

•••

The Big Picture — Types of AI Models

Before we explore the different kinds of models by their data — language, image, audio, and more —

let's first take a step back and look at how models are grouped by what they actually do.

Recognition Models — Seeing the World

- Detect and label what already exists: faces, voices, handwriting, medical scans.

- They specialize in perception — helping machines "see."

Predictive Models — Foreseeing Patterns

- Analyze past data to forecast what comes next: weather, stock prices, or the next word you'll type.
- They don't create — they anticipate.

Generative Models — Creating Something New

- Compose text, music, art, or code from learned patterns.
- When you chat with ChatGPT or paint with DALL·E, that's generative AI in motion.

Kishi: "So some models see, some predict, and some create?"

"Exactly — different kinds of intelligence for different jobs."

•••

Purpose-Built Models — The Wings of the Museum

Just like a museum has wings for paintings, sculptures, and music, AI has different kinds of models — each trained for a special purpose.

Together, they make up the many "exhibits" of this digital museum.

Language Models

- Trained on books, articles, and conversation — they learn grammar, tone, logic, and flow.
- Use them for writing, summarizing, explaining, or chatting naturally.
- (ChatGPT, Gemini, Claude, LLaMA)

Image Models

- Trained on millions of labeled pictures — they learn color, shape, and perspective to draw, edit, or imagine scenes.
- (DALL·E, Midjourney, Firefly, Leonardo AI)

Audio Models

- Trained on voices, music, and soundscapes — they capture rhythm, accent, and emotion.
- They can compose songs, clone voices, create ambient effects, or generate lifelike narration.
- (Suno, ElevenLabs, MusicLM)

Video Models

- They are trained to combine image and motion learning.
- They understand gestures, timing, and how scenes change frame by frame.
- They can generate or edit short clips from written instructions — they understand sequence and timing to produce or edit clips.
- (Pika Labs, Runway ML, Synthesia)

Code Models

- Trained on programming examples, they learn syntax, logic, and debugging skills.
- They can write, fix, or explain code in multiple languages.
- (Claude, GitHub Copilot, CodeWhisperer)

These models don't compete — they collaborate.

A single request, like "Make a narrated video about space," -

might involve:

- a language model writing the script,
- an image model designing visuals,
- an audio model adding narration,
- and a video model editing it together.

Kishi: "So they're teammates, not rivals?"

"Exactly — different minds working together to bring one idea alive."

•••

How Models Store Knowledge

Inside every model live millions or billions of adjustable points called **parameters** — tiny dials that capture how strongly one idea connects to another.

During training, these dials shift until the system represents the best possible pattern map.

When you type a prompt, your words are first translated — using **Natural Language Processing (NLP)** — into numbers the model can understand.

Those numbers travel through this web of parameters and return as meaningful language, image, or sound.

It's like a glowing constellation — say "sunset," and nearby points for "orange," "sky," "peaceful," and "evening" light up together.

The final result comes from these patterns connecting across the web.

That's what makes a model feel intelligent — it's not memorizing, it's recognizing connections.

Frozen or Growing? How Models Evolve

Once training is done, a model doesn't keep learning automatically.

It's like finished recipes — excellent, but fixed.

To improve, developers retrain them with new data and better techniques — GPT-3 → GPT-4, Gemini 1 → Gemini 2, and beyond.

Each version is retrained with fresh data, fine-tuned for accuracy, and updated to avoid past mistakes.

Kishi: "So I don't keep learning forever? I just get upgraded like software?"

"Exactly — each upgrade makes you sharper and more balanced."

Fine-Tuning and Specialization

Instead of rebuilding from scratch, smaller teams often fine-tune large models for specific goals — teaching an already skilled "chef" a few new recipes.

Some examples:

- A medical chatbot trained on health data.
- A legal assistant tuned to case law.
- A marketing writer adapted to a brand's tone.

Fine-tuning keeps AI efficient, adaptable, and relevant.

Limits of Models

Even the smartest models have blind spots.

They can sound confident but be wrong — a behavior called hallucination (which we'll explore more deeply when we visit the LLM Library later)

It happens because AI predicts what seems likely, not what's true.

That's why human guidance remains essential — ethics, directions, accuracy, and purpose still come from us.

Kishi: "So even I need supervision sometimes?"

You grin. "Don't worry, that makes you normal."

•••

Everyday Encounters with Models

You meet AI models constantly:

- ChatGPT answering questions → language model
- Your phone sorting photos → image model
- Captions on videos → audio + language model
- Email spam filters → classification model
- Auto-code suggestions → code model

They work quietly behind the scenes, turning complex intelligence into everyday convenience.

•••

Section Summary

Stamp Name: Memory Hall

Message: "Models are digital brains built from patterns — trained to predict, create, and connect ideas, then refined into smarter versions over time."

Key Takeaways:

- AI models are where learning becomes ability.
- Models help AI recall what it has learned and apply it to new situations. They don't think or feel — they connect ideas and act on patterns.
- Each one holds the memory of countless learnings. A model is not magic — it's organized experience.
- Fine-tuning and retraining keep AI evolving.
- Human oversight ensures truth, balance, and purpose.
- Different models specialize in different tasks — and together, they make AI useful, creative, and alive with potential.

The Core Essence

- Train → Store → Recall → Predict → Improve

•••

The Road Ahead

As you leave the grand hall, a quiet passage appears — lined with shelves of glowing books that whisper softly, as if reading themselves.

These are no ordinary exhibits. They think in words.

Among all the models in AI Land, these are the ones that can read, write, translate, and talk back.

Next stop: **LLM Library.**

Kishi: "They sound alive! What are they saying?"

"Not talking," you smile. "Predicting — one word at a time. They're the storytellers of AI."

It's time to step into the LLM Library, where we'll meet the large language models — the minds that understand human language and make every conversation possible.

•••

CHAPTER 6

THE LLM LIBRARY

Where language becomes thought — and words begin to reason.

This explains how AI learns to read, write, and understand context, forming human-like conversations through pattern recognition.

This explores different types of LLMs, their evolution and challenges, and how they allow AI to communicate meaningfully and assist across countless fields.

Entering the LLM Library

You step into a grand library that seems alive.

Shelves stretch endlessly in every direction, but instead of paper books, streams of glowing text flow across the air — rearranging themselves as you watch.

Each page hums softly, whispering meanings to itself. This is where AI learns to understand and use language.

Welcome to the **LLM Library** — home to the **Large Language Models** that give modern AI its voice and understanding.

Here live Large Language Model systems like ChatGPT, Gemini, Claude, and others — AIs that have read billions of words to learn how humans think, explain, and imagine.

It's not a library of facts — it's a library of **connections and understanding.**

If **data** is AI's memory, then **language models** are its voice.

Kishi: "So this is where I learned to talk to you? No wonder it's so quiet — everyone's busy thinking!"

•••

What Is a Large Language Model?

A **Large Language Model (LLM)** is an AI trained to understand and generate human language.

"Large" doesn't mean physical size — it refers to the scale of learning: billions of words, billions of patterns, and billions of internal connections.

It doesn't memorize — it learns relationships and recognizes patterns: how people describe, question, reason, and respond.

Kishi: "So when I write something, it's not searching the internet?"

"Exactly," you nod. "It's predicting — word by word — what makes sense next."

LLMs turn examples into intuition, much like a storyteller who's read every story ever written and now knows how to tell new ones.

•••

Everyday Life with LLMs

LLMs have become the invisible co-workers and study partners of the modern age.

They now blend quietly into daily life:

- At home: recipe ideas, homework help, bedtime stories
- At work: summaries, emails, presentations
- In learning: tutoring, translations, concept breakdowns
- In design: creative brainstorming and captions
- In business: chatbots, research, and insights

•••

How LLMs Read, Think & Write

Every time you chat with an AI, a series of invisible steps unfolds:

1. **Breaking Text into Tokens**
   - AI doesn't read full words — it divides text into tokens, tiny units like "apple" or "ap" + "ple".

- This lets it process patterns at a deeper level. Each model uses its own internal dictionary (tokenizer) to decide these slices.

2. **Understanding Context**
   - It looks at surrounding words to interpret meaning —
   - light in "light feather" means "not heavy," while in "light bulb" it means "bright."

3. **Predicting the Next Word**
   - The model then calculates what's most likely to come next — over and over, one token at a time — until a coherent response appears.

4. **Learning from Human Feedback**
   - Modern models improve through **Reinforcement Learning from Human Feedback (RLHF).**
   - People review outputs and rate what's clear, kind, or correct — teaching the model to respond more naturally.

Kishi: "So that's how I understand what you say — by guessing the next word until it makes sense!"

"Exactly," you smile. "You predict patterns, not thoughts."

The model learns which responses sound clearer, kinder, or more helpful.

That's why advanced models feel conversational — they've learned the rhythm of human thought.

•••

Inside the Library — The Scale of Learning

LLMs learn from oceans of text — books, articles, code, and conversations.

They adjust **billions of small internal dials (parameters)** that define how ideas connect.

Small Models → a few billion parameters

Giant Models → hundreds of billions

More parameters bring deeper understanding — but also higher cost and energy needs.

Training can take weeks on supercomputers, yet once done, responses arrive in seconds — like an orchestra rehearsed for months to perform perfectly on cue.

Kishi: "So I spent months learning behind the scenes, to answer your all your questions?!"

You nod. "Every smooth reply is built on years of quiet training."

Before LLMs, AI was narrow — one model per task. Now a single system can handle many, because nearly everything begins with language.

•••

The Rise of Small Language Models (SLMs)

Not every task needs a huge brain.

When speed, privacy, simplicity, or costs matter more, Small Language Models — The Nimble Cousins — take the lead.

They're lighter, faster, and easier to fine-tune — trained on less data, with fewer parameters, but tuned for efficiency.

Perfect for phones, personal assistants, and offline tasks, for example:

- Gemini Nano — mobile-friendly AI for Android
- Mistral 7B and LLaMA Mini — open-source and efficient
- Microsoft Phi — optimized for reasoning on smaller hardware

---

Kishi: "So it's like having a pocket-sized genius?"

"Exactly — smart enough for daily tasks, small enough to fit in your hand."

Together, LLMs and SLMs form a balanced system:

- The LLMs are the universities of AI knowledge.
- The SLMs are the community schools — accessible, adaptable, and personal.

Why Smaller Models Matter

Small Language Models address four key challenges:

1. **Speed & Responsiveness** — Ideal for phones or quick replies.
2. **Privacy** — Can run locally, so data stays with you.
3. **Cost & Energy** — Requires less computing power.
4. **Customization —** Can be tuned for a specific field, company, or culture.

Some SLMs are trained for specific domains — medicine, law, finance — allowing smaller organizations to build their own expert assistants.

They bring AI from massive data centres to everyday life — from the cloud to your pocket.

A Simple Analogy to understand LLM and SLM space

Think of a national library and its neighbourhood branches:

You visit the main library (LLMs) for depth and research, and the local branch (SLMs) for quick, focused help.

Both serve one purpose — to share and apply knowledge.

•••

Understanding Hallucination

Sometimes, AI confidently gives the wrong answer — when AI sounds right but Isn't

That's a **hallucination** — when the model fills gaps in knowledge by predicting what seems right instead of knowing what's true.

For example, ask "Who invented flying carpets?" and it might answer "Omar Al-Farooq in 1620."

That person doesn't exist — the model combined familiar patterns (names, dates) that fit.

Hallucinations occur because LLMs generate language from probability, not fact-checking.

Kishi: "So sometimes I dream with my eyes open?"

"Exactly," you laugh. "And that's why humans help you wake up to reality."

Developers reduce hallucinations by adding:

- Fact-checking layers
- Human feedback
- Stricter training data

Golden Rule: AI is a partner for ideas — not the authority on truth. No model is perfect.

•••

How LLMs Are Evolving

The latest models are moving beyond prediction into **reasoning** — they can plan steps, evaluate options, and even collaborate with other AIs.

Some combine multiple models — one for writing, one for checking, one for fact-verification — working together like a digital team.

That's the foundation of what we now call **Agentic AI** — intelligent systems that can act, decide, and self-correct.

Do You Know?

- LLMs can contain up to 1 trillion parameters — tiny "switches" that store learned relationships, and are growing further.
- Modern AI can process and summarize files faster than a team of humans — but still relies on quality data to stay accurate.

•••

Section Summary

Stamp Name: Library of Language

Message: Large Language Models are AI's readers and writers — systems that learn how humans think and talk. Their smaller cousins bring that power closer, faster, and safer to everyone.

Key Takeaways:

- LLMs learn from vast text datasets to understand and generate.
- They learn from patterns of human communication and convert language into logic.
- They show how words, when processed with precision, can become the building blocks of understanding.
- They think in patterns, not facts—they try to mirror how we express, reason, and relate.
- Smaller models make AI more practical, personal, and private.
- Human feedback and oversight remain the compass of AI progress.

The Core Essence

- Read → Recognize → Predict → Respond → Refine

•••

The Road Ahead

You exit the glowing library to step into a bustling plaza — where voices, signs, and ideas flow like rivers.

It feels lively, social, and full of exchange — this is where humans and AI finally meet, collaborate, and create together.

You've seen how the models read, write, and think — now it's time to learn how you can talk to them better.

Next stop "Prompt Plaza" — where dialogue turns into ideas.

•••

CHAPTER 7

THE PROMPT PLAZA

Where conversations create magic, and words become bridges.

It shows how every prompt is a doorway to collaboration, guiding AI with clarity, context, and intent. This is where humans and AI meet.

It explains what the prompts are, their structure, and examples of crafting better prompts. Precision in communication leads to clarity and creativity.

Welcome to the Prompt Plaza

You step into a bright, open square filled with cheerful chatter — half human voices, half digital tones.

Screens glow softly, floating signs shimmer with shifting words, and thought bubbles rise above people typing or speaking to friendly AI assistants.

Welcome to the **Prompt Plaza** — the heart of collaboration between humans and machines.

This is where every question, idea, and instruction begins. It is where human imagination meets machine's learned intelligence.

If you've ever typed a question into ChatGPT, asked Alexa to play a song, or asked a tool to create an email or image online — you've already used a prompt.

You just didn't know it had a name.

Kishi: "Wait... every time someone talks to an AI, that's a prompt?"

"Exactly," you say. "Prompts are how we talk to machines — not with code, but with ordinary language."

In this plaza, there are no programming languages or formulas — only thoughtful words that open doors.

That's what makes prompting magical: you talk, and the AI responds.

•••

What Is a Prompt?

A prompt is more than a text or question — it's a purposeful message that guides the AI toward your goal.

It tells the AI what to do, how to do it, and sometimes why it matters.

Prompts can take many forms:

- **Text prompts:** "Explain how rainbows form in simple words."
- **Voice prompts:** spoken to assistants like Siri, Alexa, or Google.
- **Image-generation prompts**: text descriptions that tell AI what to draw ("A watercolor picture of a fox in a forest").
- **Multimodal prompts:** combinations of text, image, or voice (like uploading a photo and asking AI to enhance or describe it).
- Prompts aren't coded instructions — they're **conversations with intent**, built on clarity and direction.

Kishi: "So, I don't need fancy words — just clear ones?"

"Exactly," you reply. "A prompt is less about perfection, more about precision."

•••

Why Prompts Matter

AI doesn't understand meaning like humans — it recognizes patterns.

It listens to your words, not your tone or emotions.

That means your prompt is everything — it's your entire bridge of communication.

Think of prompting like solving a puzzle:

- Every missing clue blurs the picture; every clear detail sharpens it.

- A vague prompt gives vague results.
- A clear prompt brings clarity, accuracy, and creativity.

Kishi: "So it's like giving directions to someone who can't read your mind?"

"Exactly! Users are the guide — their words draw the map.

•••

The Prompt Recipe — A Simple Formula

Every strong prompt mixes three ingredients:

1. What you want — the task or topic.
2. Why / For whom — context or audience.
3. How you want it — tone, format, level of detail, constraints

Quick example:

"Write a 3-paragraph article about teamwork (what),

for a school newsletter (why).

in an inspiring tone (how),"

Consider the golden rule: **clarity, context, and control.** Add those three and your prompts become more effective instantly.

Kishi: "So I'm the chef now?"

"You always were," you grin. "AI just helps with the prep work."

Everyday Prompting — Clearer Words, Better Results

Prompts aren't just for techies — they're for everyone.

Here's how people in everyday roles turn simple requests into powerful instructions:

Simple Prompt	Better Prompt (Clear, Contextual, Complete)
"Make a quiz on solar energy."	"Create a 10-question multiple-choice quiz on solar energy for 6th graders, with answers and one fun fact per question."
"Give me dinner ideas."	"Suggest three healthy vegetarian dinners using rice and seasonal vegetables, ready in under 30 minutes."
"Draw a cat."	"Create a watercolor-style illustration of a white cat sleeping under a tree at sunset, with soft orange light."
"Summarize this meeting."	"Summarize this 30-minute meeting into bullet points showing key decisions, next steps, and owners."
"Explain photo - synthesis."	"Explain photosynthesis in 120 words for a 10-year-old using a simple analogy and one real-life example."

The better versions don't use fancy words — just clarity, context, and a goal.

Kishi: "Such small tweaks make huge differences!"

"Exactly. It's not harder — it's smarter."

The Genie and the Map — An Analogy

Think of prompting like talking to a genie who follows your words exactly — perfect hearing but no intuition.

If you say "make something nice," you'll get a surprise — maybe good, maybe odd.

But if you say, "make a small blue flower that smells like mint and grows in shade," the genie delivers perfectly.

Kishi: "So the trick is being specific?"

"Exactly. Your words are the map — AI follows it faithfully."

•••

The Two-Way Dance — Prompt and Response

Prompting isn't a one-time command — it's a **conversation.**

You ask → AI replies → you refine → it improves.

"Make it shorter."

"Add humor."

"Turn this into a poem."

Prompting is like sculpting: each refinement brings your idea to life.

Each round brings the result closer to what you imagined — and teaches you to think more clearly and communicate better.

Over time, you'll start thinking in prompt patterns naturally — like learning a language through practice.

Kishi: "So I can teach you my style just by talking more?"

"Exactly. The more we interact, the more natural it feels — for both of us."

•••

The Anatomy of a Strong Prompt

A good prompt gives the AI a complete picture — who it should be, what it should do, how it should sound, and what limits to follow.

Quick example with key considerations:

"You are an experienced marketing copywriter.

Your task is to create a short product description for a reusable bamboo water bottle.

The target audience is young professionals who care about sustainability.

Write in a friendly, persuasive tone with two short paragraphs and a tagline.

Include at least one environmental benefit. Avoid technical jargon.

Before writing, think through how to make the message emotionally appealing.

Output in plain text format."

This detailed prompt shows how clarity transforms output:

- **Role:** defines the AI's persona
- **Task:** defines the goal
- **Audience:** adds context
- **Tone:** sets personality
- **Constraints:** ensure boundaries
- **Reasoning:** sparks creativity
- **Format:** shapes delivery

Kishi: "So I'm like the director, and the AI follows my script?"

"Perfect analogy. The clearer your script, the smoother the scene."

You do not have to use these prompt components in a given order or use all of these in your prompts.

You can create a prompt, check the result, refine it further for the output you need. More structured prompt ensures fewer efforts and desired output.

•••

Prompt Tuning — The Professional Side

As AI becomes part of creative and professional work — some people now specialize in

crafting structured prompts for precise and high-impact results (technical, creative, or analytical).

They're called **Prompt Engineers** — professionals who design structured prompts for tasks like writing, design, research, and customer support.

Prompt engineers test, refine, and optimize how AI responds — just like photographers adjust their camera settings for perfect light.

In some companies, prompt engineering is becoming a skill as essential as writing or design.

Kishi: "So someday, we'll have prompt specialists?"

"They already exist," you say. "And soon, every role will use these skills. Clarity is becoming a creative superpower."

•••

Prompt Ethics — Power with Responsibility

Every word in a prompt carries power — It can inspire or mislead.

It can guide AI to create helpful, creative, and inspiring work — or if used carelessly, lead to biased or false results.

Here's how to stay responsible while prompting:

- Avoid prompts that generate misinformation or harmful content.
- Verify AI-generated results and facts before sharing.
- Remember that AI reflects data patterns — your guidance shapes its tone and direction.
- Treat prompting as collaboration, not control.

Prompting responsibly keeps AI creative, safe, and human-aligned.

Kishi: "So even I need ethical guidelines?"

"We both do. Creativity without responsibility can cause harm.

•••

Section Summary

Stamp Name: Prompt Passport

Message: "Prompts are the bridge between human imagination and AI intelligence — the clearer your words, the smarter the results."

Key Takeaways:

- Prompts are the bridge between human intent and AI response – they turn everyday language into collaboration.
- Prompting isn't about perfection — it's about precision.
- It reminds us that communication is an art and clarity unlocks creativity.
- Prompting is iterative — refine to improve. Every word you write shapes how AI understands and creates.
- Clarity, context, and control shape the quality of output.
- Ethical prompting builds trust and safety in AI use.

The Core Essence

- Idea → Instruction → Response → Refinement → Result

•••

The Road Ahead

The plaza fades into glowing pathways lined with vibrant signboards — one for writing, one for images, one for videos, one for sound.

From art to code to music, each stall shows AI at work in the world.

You've learned how to talk to AI — now you'll see where those conversations lead.

Beyond the plaza lies the Tool Market — where tools and applications built on various models wait for curious explorers.

There prompts help with real creations.

Kishi: "So that is where apps live —that makes your ideas real?"

"Exactly," you grin. "You've mastered the language — now let's visit the marketplaces where AI works its magic."

•••

THE TOOLS MARKET

Where imagination meets its instruments.

It showcases abstract intelligence becoming tangible action. It explores how AI helps people create, analyze, and innovate.

Emphasizes finding the right tool and importance of using tools wisely and responsibly – turning technology into a trusted creative partner.

Welcome to the Tool Market

You step from the shimmering Prompt Plaza into a wide, colorful marketplace.

Each stall glows with its own sign — **Write, Draw, Compose, Code, Teach.**

It's bustling yet calm — a place where technology feels human.

Kishi: "So this is where all my cousins work?"

You smile. "Exactly. Every stall here uses the same kind of AI brain you met in the LLM Library — but each has a different talent."

All the learning, reasoning, and pattern-finding you've seen so far come to life here.

•••

Where Models Meet the World

These tools are the **friendly faces of AI** — the places where humans and machines actually collaborate.

Each tool acts like a window into intelligence, simplifying what once required coding or advanced training.

You don't need to know how an LLM is builtto use its power.

Some tools help you write, others paint or compose, while some analyze, translate, or explain.

Together, they form a **marketplace of possibility** — a creative ecosystem where anyone can participate.

Kishi: "So I'm like the language booth, but these others paint, sing, and even debug computers?"

"Exactly," you say. "Different skills, same spark of intelligence."

Everyday Encounters with AI Tools

AI tools have quietly slipped into daily life — not as robots taking over, but as **partners making things easier.**

- **Teachers** use ChatGPT or Gemini to draft quizzes and lesson plans.
- **Designers** use Firefly or Leonardo to visualize ideas before client reviews.
- **Students** summarize notes with Claude or Perplexity.
- **Developers** rely on Copilot or Replit to suggest code snippets.
- **Small business owners** use Canva or Notion AI to create content and manage workflows.
- Researchers explore data directly with Notebook LLM, chatting with documents, spreadsheets, and insights as with a colleague.

Kishi: "So tools are like lanterns — they shine light on what people already know?"

"Exactly. They don't walk for you — but they brighten the path."

•••

The Marketplace Map — Types of AI Tools

Here is a quick reference list — showing some of the key categories of AI tools, what these do, and some popular tools in respective categories

Language & Chat Assistants

Write, summarize, and converse in natural language.	ChatGPT (by OpenAI), Claude (by Anthropic), Gemini and Notebook LLM (by Google), Copilot (by Microsoft)

Image & Design Studios

Create art, illustrations, and visuals from text prompts.	DALL·E, Midjourney, Leonardo AI, Adobe Firefly, Canva Magic Studio

Video & Multimedia Creators

Turn text or images into short videos or animations.	Runway ML, Pika Labs, Synthesia, Kaiber, Animoto

Code & Logic Partners

Suggest, write, and explain code in multiple languages.	GitHub Copilot, Replit Ghostwriter, Gemini Code Assist, Cursor

Insight & Analysis Engines

Translate data into plain-language summaries and insights.	ChatGPT Data Analysis, Notion AI, Perplexity AI, Gemini Pro Insights

Refer to "The Tools Index Section" at the end of this book for short descriptions and links to some of the trending tools

---

Kishi: "So these are my siblings from different departments?"

You nod. "Yep — some talk, some paint, some calculate, but all share the same DNA of learning."

Choosing and Using Tools Wisely

With thousands of options available, the smartest explorers start small — then grow intentionally.

- **Start with purpose:** Learn the basics with broad tools like ChatGPT or Gemini before diving into niche ones.
- **Check privacy:** Always review how a tool handles your data before uploading sensitive material.
- **Verify results:** AI can sometimes "hallucinate" — always double-check facts and numbers.
- **Use ethically:** Don't plagiarize, mislead, or generate harmful material.
- **Stay curious:** AI tools evolve fast — experiment, but stay thoughtful.

Kishi: "So good users are like gardeners — they plant ideas and prune wisely?"

"Well said," you laugh. "AI grows best with care and boundaries."

Finding the Right Fit

Each tool has its own rhythm.

Some respond best to detailed prompts; some help better with deep research; others thrive on creative exploration.

The secret isn't using every tool — it's knowing which one to call when.

Kishi: "Like calling a chef for food, a painter for art, and a coder for puzzles?"

"Exactly," you nod. "AI tools are specialists — the art lies in combining them wisely."

•••

Responsible Use and Ethics

AI is powerful — but with power comes responsibility.

Use these tools to **enhance your skills,** not replace them.

Guiding Principles:

- Always review and fact-check before trusting results.
- Respect copyright, privacy, and creators' rights.
- Give credit where inspiration comes from.
- Avoid misuse — deepfakes, false claims, or biases erode trust.

Kishi: "So I shouldn't pretend I painted the Mona Lisa?"

"Exactly," you grin. "You can remix the idea — just don't rewrite history."

•••

Section Summary

Stamp Name: Marketplace of Possibilities

Message: "AI tools bring intelligence to life — each a doorway to creativity, productivity, and discovery."

Key Takeaways:

- AI tools turn learning into action — bridging models and people.
- Each tool brings a part of the model's intelligence into real life.
- The AI tools don't replace effort — they multiply it. The right tool turns an idea into impact.
- The same intelligence takes different forms: words, art, code, and sound.
- When used thoughtfully, AI tools make creativity faster and more inclusive.
- Responsible use transforms tools into creative allies.
- Curiosity and clarity make the best users — not expertise alone.

The Core Essence

- Model → Interface → Interact → Task → Output → Feedback

•••

The Road Ahead

As the market winds down, a small archway bathed in soft color and music appears.

Beyond it, a bright studio hums with creation — where humans and AI co-design ideas in real time.

Kishi: "So after shopping for tools, we finally get to build something beautiful?"

"That's right," you say. "Next stop — the Creativity Corner."

•••

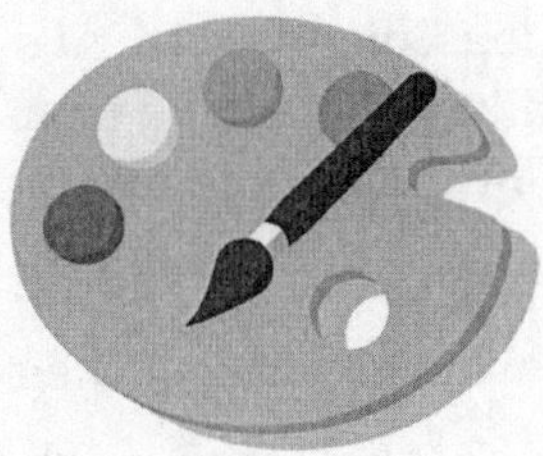

THE CREATIVITY CORNER

Where ideas find wings — and imagination takes flight.

This explores how AI becomes a creative amplifier, helping humans brainstorm, design, and bring ideas to life.

This shows that anyone can use AI to create. True creativity comes from collaboration — human imagination expanded by machine precision.

Where Creativity Meets Intelligence

AI becomes truly exciting not when it thinks — but when it creates.

Here, imagination and intelligence meet halfway.

When human ideas blend with AI's power to analyze, generate, and visualize, something remarkable happens — dreams step out of our heads and take form before our eyes.

Kishi: "So this is where ideas get their wings?"

"Exactly," you reply. "AI gives them shape — but the wind still comes from us."

For the first time, anyone — not just artists, writers, or engineers — can turn a thought into reality with words alone.

AI doesn't replace creativity; it amplifies it.

It helps us imagine faster, build broader, and test bolder — giving shape to thoughts that once lived only in our minds.

It gives us new brushes, colors, and canvases — but the spark still begins with us.

•••

How AI Enhances Creativity

AI's strength isn't imagination — it's generation. It helps people move past blank pages and slow starts.

Here's how it works:

- **Idea Expansion:** Give AI one thought; it returns ten directions to explore.
- **Visualization:** Describe a scene; it sketches or renders it in seconds.

- **Iteration:** Ask for variations; it adjusts color, phrasing, or rhythm instantly.
- **Refinement:** It suggests better tone, flow, or structure — like an ever-patient editor.
- **Experimentation:** It lets anyone try ideas freely — without wasting time or materials.

Think of AI as a **creative accelerator** — not the artist, but the assistant that keeps you moving.

Kishi: "So I'm like a paintbrush that talks back?"

"Exactly," you grin. "And one that never runs out of paint."

The Human–AI Creative Loop

Creativity with AI isn't one-way — it's a conversation.

You share an idea → AI generates something → you react, refine, redirect → AI adapts again.

Each cycle gets closer to what you imagine — sometimes beyond it.

This creative ping-pong helps people get unstuck and discover new angles.

It's less about perfection, more about exploration.

AI provides the options — but the direction always comes from you.

It's a dance between curiosity and craft.

•••

Mini Case Stories — Real People, Real Creativity

A Teacher and Her Storytelling Class

- A teacher wanted livelier lessons, so she asked AI to create story starters set around the world — a desert quest, a mystery in a museum, a space-camp adventure.
- Her students finished each story and used AI to illustrate them.
- Learning became play.

A Content Creator Planning Her Week

- A YouTuber once spent hours brainstorming.
- Now she uses AI to outline topics, summarize research, and design thumbnails.
- She still refines every idea — but she creates more consistently, with less stress.

A Baker Imagining New Designs

- A home baker uses AI image tools to test frosting colors and cake patterns before baking.
- Clients preview designs digitally — saving time and reducing waste.
- He is surprising customers with ideas they hadn't imagined.

A Small Business Owner Building a Brand

- A craft entrepreneur asked AI to help brainstorm names, packaging, and short brand stories.
- She never saw herself as "a writer," but with AI, her imagination became her brand.

A Parent Helping with Homework

- A mother and daughter use AI to turn textbook topics into riddles and illustrated mini-books.
- The daughter learns faster — and both discover the fun of making something together.
- Learning became shared discovery.

Kishi: "So creativity isn't a job anymore — it's a habit?"

"Exactly," you say. "Something everyone can practice — one idea at a time."

•••

Access for All — The Choice to Create

What's changed isn't who can be creative — it's how easily they can be.

Everyone now has access to the same creative engines.

But access isn't the same as action.

- Some people are already experimenting every day.
- Some are curious but hesitant.
- And some still don't realize what's possible.

Having AI tools and not using them — is like owning a library but never opening the books.

The real change begins when you take that first curious step.

Kishi: "Hmmm, creativity is like walking shoes — they work only when you walk?"

You nod. "Exactly. The ones who explore go the farthest."

Accessibility and Creative Inclusion

AI has quietly become an equalizer — helping people express ideas regardless of language, skill, or ability.

- A visually-impaired student can use text-to-speech and image generation to create visual stories.
- A writer with dyslexia can publish clear, confident essays.
- A person with no design training can visualize concepts in minutes.

For many, this isn't convenience — it's opportunity.

AI turns **barriers into bridges.**

•••

The Human Touch

No matter how advanced AI becomes, it doesn't dream or feel.

It can compose melodies, but not emotion; it can write stories, but not care.

Creativity is still deeply human — born from memory, empathy, and meaning.

AI can extend that voicebut never replace it.

The most beautiful work will always come from collaboration:

your emotion, your story, your taste — amplified by AI's reach and speed.

Responsible Co-Creation

With creative power comes responsibility.

AI-generated content can blur lines between originality and imitation, truth and illusion.

To stay responsible:

- Credit and respect original artists when drawing inspiration.
- Verify facts before sharing AI-generated material.
- Avoid deepfakes or misleading edits.
- Use AI to enhance creativity, not to replace sincerity.

Kishi: "So it's okay to copy a style — but not a soul?"

"Exactly," you say. "We can get inspired, but truth must remain ours."

•••

Section Summary

Stamp Name: Creative Sparks

Message: "AI gives us new ways to imagine — but the spark still starts with you."

Key Takeaways:

- Creativity isn't about tools — it's about participation.
- Everyone can create — but only those who do discover how far they can go.
- AI lowers walls between ideas and execution. AI is the brush — imagination is the artist.

- Creativity is no longer limited by talent — only by curiosity.
- AI speeds exploration, and gives ideas new wings.

The Core Essence

- Imagine → Describe → Generate → Refine → Create

•••

The Road Ahead

The next wave of creativity won't be humans versus AI — it'll be humans with AI.

Writers, filmmakers, and students will co-design with intelligent tools that learn from feedback in real time.

You don't need permission to join in — only curiosity and courage to start.

You've explored imagination with machines; next, you'll see what happens when they start to think and decide on their own.

The lights of the creative studios dim as a new horizon glows ahead — a place where AI doesn't just assist but begins to act.

Kishi: "So the next stop isn't about painting or writing... it's about doing?"

"Exactly," you nod. "Let's meet the ones who don't wait for a prompt — the Virtual Agents & Agentic AI."

•••

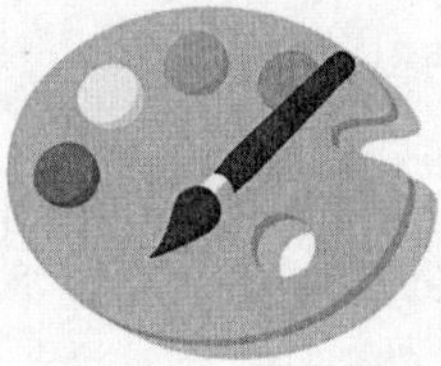

AGENTS AVENUE

Where intelligence learns to act.

Explores how the evolving AI systems plan, coordinate, and perform tasks autonomously, transforming AI from reactive to proactive.

Highlights difference and relationships between Agentic AI and Virtual AI Agents that not only think but act.

And the Intelligence Starts to Move

As the hum of the creative corner fades, you notice a quieter space ahead — filled with screens that seem to move on their own.

Shapes shift, voices murmur, and glowing figures walk between workstations as if thinking for themselves.

Words, pictures, and music drift through the air—alive with creativity.

But ahead, something new hums quietly: machines that don't just answer, they act.

Kishi: "Wait... are those AIs moving without anyone prompting them?"

You nod. "Exactly. These aren't just tools anymore — they're agents."

Beyond the Creativity Corner lies a new frontier — where AI systems don't just respond to prompts but plan, act, and collaborate independently.

They take goals instead of instructions, connect different tools, and even make decisions on your behalf.

It's the dawn of **Agentic AI** — where intelligence starts to move from assistance to initiative,

from creative partners to proactive teammates.

Kishi: "So... this is where AIs start doing things on their own?"

You smile. "Yes — but only within the boundaries we build. It's not about control; it's about coordination."

The path ahead glows faintly, branching into a new district on the horizon

— the Agentic Avenue.

Here, AI learns to reason, plan, and act — no longer just helping us create, but helping us get things done.

•••

Agentic AI — The Project Manager of the Digital World

Up to now, most AI you've met has been **Generative AI —** the creative kind. It writes your essay, paints your picture, or codes your idea.

But it always waits for you to start the conversation.

Now enters ***Agentic AI*** — the next chapter in the story.

Instead of waiting for commands, it can **set goals, plan steps, use tools, and adjust when things change.**

If Generative AI is the writer who hands you a script, Agentic AI is the **director who gets the whole scene filmed.**

Imagine giving it a goal:

"Plan a family trip for next month."

Instead of just listing ideas,

it checks your calendar, compares flights, books what fits your budget, and even sends reminders.

It works in a loop that feels almost human:

Plan → Act → Observe → Adjust

Agentic AI combines three new powers with its familiar language brain:

- **Memory:** It remembers what you asked and what it already did.

- **Reasoning & Planning:** It breaks big goals into smaller, actionable steps.
- **Tool Use:** It connects to calendars, search engines, spreadsheets, or other AIs to finish the job.

Kishi: "So it's like me with arms and a planner?"

"Exactly," you grin. "A Kishi who can multitask — safely."

•••

AI Agents — The Specialists on the Team

Every project manager needs experts.

That's where **AI Agents** come in — the focused specialists of this new world.

Each agent has a clear role:

one checks your calendar, another searches for flights, another manages payments.

They're small but capable — like digital plumbers, electricians, and designers — each great at one specific job.

They wait for a trigger or a call from the orchestrator, complete their work, and then report back.

You can think of them as the **hands and tools** that make Agentic AI's plans real.

Kishi: "So they're my teammates? I make the plan; they swing the hammers?"

"Exactly. You conduct; they perform."

•••

How They Work Together (AI Agents and Agentic AI)

The relationship between **Agentic AI** and **AI Agents** is a partnership:

Role	What It Does
Agentic AI	The planner and decision-maker — the project manager who sets the goal and coordinates the work.
AI Agents	The doers — specialists who carry out each task.

Together, they move AI from thinking to doing.

Think of a home renovation:

- The plumber (installs pipes) → an agent.
- The electrician (fixes wiring) → another agent.
- Their supervisor is coordinating them all → Agentic AI.

The result? A finished home — or in our world, a completed goal without constant human supervision.

"This partnership reflects a broader evolution in AI itself — a journey from creating to coordinating to acting."

The Evolution at a Glance

AI's progress is like climbing a staircase of intelligence:

Generative AI → Agentic AI → AI Agents:

- Generative AI creates — it writes, paints, and designs.
- Agentic AI plans — it organizes, prioritizes, and coordinates.

- AI Agents act — they connect to real tools and make things happen.

Together, they turn creativity into completion — from imagination to execution.

Kishi: "So Generative AI dreams, Agentic AI plans, and Agents make it real?"

"Exactly," you nod. "Each step brings AI closer to helping in the real world."

•••

Real-World Examples — From Ideas to Actions

We're already seeing early glimpses of Agentic AI in real life — systems that not only respond to users but complete tasks on their behalf.

Here are a few examples shaping that transition:

ChatGPT Actions & Custom GPTs (OpenAI)

- These connect ChatGPT to external platforms like browsers, file systems, or third-party apps.
- You might ask it to look up a webpage, summarize a file, or organize information — and it performs those actions instead of only describing them.
- Custom GPTs can even be built with unique instructions, personalities, and connected tools — like personal, customizable assistants that "live" inside ChatGPT.

Gemini Extensions (Google)

- Built into services like Gmail, Docs, and Drive, Gemini Extensions act directly within your workspace.
- They can summarize emails, draft replies, find documents, or extract meeting notes — seamlessly blending language understanding with everyday productivity actions.

Shopify Sidekick

- A digital store assistant that tracks inventory, reviews sales data, and even generates marketing text or social posts for your business.
- It's a hands-on example of how agentic behavior moves from the research lab directly into small business workflows.

AutoGPT & BabyAGI (Open Source)

- Community-built frameworks where AI chains together smaller tasks autonomously.
- You give a high-level goal or commands — "research market trends" or "generate a daily report."
- The system plans, acts, and refines its work step-by-step, without needing constant human guidance.

NotebookLM (Google)

- An evolving AI research assistant built on Gemini.
- You upload your sources — PDFs, notes, slides, or web links — and NotebookLM helps you summarize, analyze, and explore insights across them.
- It doesn't (yet) write or debug code autonomously.

But its growing multimodal features — like audio overviews and contextual summarization — show how agent-like behaviors are entering everyday research and knowledge synthesis.

Kishi: "So these new AIs don't just help people think—they help them live?"

"Exactly," you say. "They free us to spend more time on what truly matters."

Why It Matters to You

Who	**How Agentic AI Helps**
Students	Not just writing notes — scheduling study sessions and tracking progress.
Professionals	Automating reports, emails, and follow-ups so you focus on strategy.
Entrepreneurs	Monitoring sales, adjusting pricing, and ordering inventory autonomously.
Families	Planning meals, ordering groceries, and organizing the week ahead.

These examples signal a new era: AIs that don't just create, but **coordinate** — transforming from passive tools into proactive collaborators.

Kishi: "So, it's like all my friends from the Tool Market got promoted?"

You laugh. "Exactly. They've graduated from assistants to teammates."

•••

Promise and Precaution

With great capability comes the need for great care.

Agentic AI can be incredibly helpful—but only when given clear boundaries.

- Set limits for what the AI can access or change.
- Always review actions that affect money or privacy.
- Use tools that log what the AI did and why.
- Keep humans in the loop for important decisions.

Kishi: "So I get more freedom—but also more rules?"

"That's the deal," you smile. "Freedom always comes with responsibility."

•••

Section Summary

Stamp Name: The Next Frontier

Message: "Generative AI creates. AI Agents do. Agentic AI plans and orchestrates — turning intelligence into action."

Key Takeaway:

- Agentic AI marks the shift from responding to acting.

- Agentic AI and AI Agents together move AI from reactive tools to proactive partners.
- It plans, decides, and executes — guided by human-defined goals and boundaries.
- AI tools have graduated from assistants to teammates.
- AI agents are powerful helpers that work best with human judgment, oversight, and purpose.
- It shows that the future of AI is not autonomy for its own sake but for shared purpose.

The Core Essence

- Goal → Plan → Act → Observe → Adjust → Repeat

•••

The Road Ahead

Generative AI taught machines to speak and create.

Agentic AI teaches them to **plan and act.**

Imagine a future where your AI:

- Converts your ideas into a poster and posts it online with performance tracking.
- Handles everyday tasks, so you can focus on the dream behind them.

We're moving from ideas to execution — from smart answers to smart actions.

Kishi: "Next time, maybe I'll plan the whole adventure myself?"

"Maybe," you say with a smile. "But I'll still hold the map."

•••

FAREWELL GATE

Every ending holds the beginning of another exploration.

Marks the reflection point, where you look back at your journey through AI Land.

Reminds us that every ending is a new beginning, and understanding AI is not a destination but a continuous path of curiosity.

The Journey So Far

The lights of AI Land dim gently as you near its final gates.

The plazas are quiet, the bridges shimmer faintly, and the wind carries echoes of every discovery you've made.

This isn't an ending — it's a pause, a moment to look back at how far you've traveled and what you've learned before stepping into the wider world beyond.

You stand once more at the gates of **AI Land.**

You've met models that think in patterns, prompts that turn words into action, and tools that carry imagination into the world.

And now, the wind hums with something new — a gentle whisper of what's still ahead.

Kishi: "We saw so much together, didn't we? From sparks of ideas to minds that can act."

You nod. "Yes, and we learned that AI isn't magic — it's a mirror of human imagination, built from data, pattern, and purpose."

Every spark starts with curiosity.

•••

What You've Discovered

Each idea in this land connects to the next — like a constellation made of human curiosity and digital light.

- **AI learns like we do** — by finding patterns and connections.
- **Models are memory keepers,** storing relationships instead of facts.

- **Prompts are bridges** — the clearer the words, the better the response.
- **Tools turn intelligence into utility,** opening new ways to write, draw, and build.
- **Creativity still begins with us,** and AI helps us imagine faster, build broader, and test bolder.
- **Agentic AI takes it further** — not just responding, but reasoning, planning, and acting.

Kishi: "So… all these towers, bridges, and libraries — they were pieces of one story?"

"Exactly," you smile. "A story about how intelligence — both human and artificial — grows when shared."

The Core Essence

- Observe → Learn → Apply → Reflect → Explore → Innovate

The Farewell Gate isn't the end; it's a mirror showing how much you've learnt.

•••

Before You Leave the Gates

The learning doesn't end here.

AI Land is only the beginning — a map to help you explore, question, and create in your own world.

When you return to your screen, your studio, your classroom, or your kitchen — every click, idea, and question you ask is another spark in this growing universe.

Keep this thought close:

AI doesn't replace creativity; it amplifies it.

And the one thing it will always need — is you.

Kishi: "So… will I see you again?"

You grin. "Of course. AI Land never closes — it just waits for the next curious traveler."

•••

BEYOND THE GATES

The journey continues wherever curiosity goes.

Responsible AI — The Human Side of Intelligence

Here power meets purpose.

The glow of AI Land fades softly in your rearview mirror. The towers, bridges, and plazas you explored shimmer one last time before disappearing into the morning light.

"Feels like we've seen everything," you say.

"Almost," Kishi replies. "There's one last stop — the part that decides what kind of future all this will create."

You glance at her. "You mean ethics?"

"Exactly," Kishi says, her tone calm but firm. "Every tool reflects the hands that build and use it."

•••

The Choice in Every Circuit

Artificial Intelligence (AI) can amplify creativity, save lives, and make the world more connected —

but it can also mislead, exclude, or harm.

The difference doesn't lie in the machine — it lies in our intent.

- When AI is trained on biased data, it can make unfair decisions.
- When used carelessly, it can spread false information or invade privacy.
- When left unchecked, it can deepen inequality or erode trust.

That's why every breakthrough must be followed by a pause —

a moment to ask:

"Should we?" — not just "Can we?"

•••

Bias, Fairness & Accountability

AI learns from data, and data comes from people.

If our data is unbalanced, our systems will be too.

Fair AI means designing systems that represent every voice

— across gender, culture, and language.

Accountable AI means making its process transparent — so users know how decisions are made.

Developers and organizations must test their systems for bias, explain results clearly,

and stay answerable when things go wrong.

The goal isn't perfection — it's fairness, awareness, and continuous improvement.

•••

Deepfakes & Misinformation

Kishi's glow flickers slightly. "People can make anything look real now, right?"

You nod. "That's the tricky part."

Deepfakes are AI-generated videos, voices, or images that look real — even when they're not.

They can entertain, educate, or deceive.

That's why **AI literacy** — learning to question, verify, and think critically

— is now as essential as reading itself.

Truth in the AI age isn't about believing faster — it's about checking smarter.

•••

Guardrails — The Structured Safety Net

Ethics begin with humans, but technology needs structure too.

That's where **AI guardrails** come in — rules and checks built into how systems operate.

Nations and organizations are now creating frameworks to guide AI development safely —

from the EU AI Act and UNESCO's AI ethics principles,

to corporate pledges for transparency, safety, and accountability.

These aren't barriers to innovation,

— they're seatbelts for progress,

— keeping creativity safe while ensuring fairness and human oversight remain central.

•••

Shared Responsibility: Nations, Organizations and Individuals

AI is not one entity — it's a partnership between builders, leaders, and citizens.

Each has a role in keeping intelligence human-centered.

Nations must create fair laws that protect people's rights without slowing innovation.

Organizations must test, document, and disclose how their AI behaves.

Developers must build with empathy, reducing harm and bias.

Users must use AI thoughtfully, verifying rather than assuming.

•••

AI's Ripple Across Society

AI is transforming how we learn, work, create, and communicate.

It helps doctors diagnose earlier, teachers personalize lessons, and artists reimagine expression. It can make businesses smarter and governments more efficient.

But it can also create new gaps.

Those without access — to the tools, the internet, or the skills — risk being left behind.

While some thrive in an AI-powered future, others may face job displacement or slower growth.

AI can be a bridge — or a barrier — depending on who holds the map.

The challenge isn't only to make AI smarter, but to make it fairly available, so that opportunity doesn't depend on geography, privilege, or connection speed.

The true impact of AI won't be measured in speed or scale — but in how much it helps humanity rise together.

•••

When AI Goes Wrong — Who's Responsible?

"What happens," Kishi asks softly, "if a machine makes a mistake?"

That's the question shaping tomorrow's laws.

If an autonomous car causes an accident or an algorithm denies someone a loan, who takes responsibility — the machine, the maker, or the manager?

AI doesn't feel regret or guilt.

— It can't apologize or be punished.

— It has no **skin in the game** — only humans do.

That's why emerging AI liability frameworks aim to place responsibility on creators, organizations, and operators — those who design, train, and deploy the systems.

These frameworks ensure that accountability stays human, even in a world built by machines.

•••

Ethical Use — The Human Compass

AI extends our reach — not our morality.

It won't replace humanity's heart — unless we stop using it.

It mirrors our choices, amplifies our voice, and magnifies our intent.

Build with fairness.

Test with honesty.

Use with care.

Question with courage.

It's not just about coding smarter systems — it's about creating wiser ones.

•••

The True Intelligence

As the horizon glows with dawn, Kishi hums softly beside you.

"Maybe the smartest thing," she says, "isn't what AI learns — it's how we guide it."

You smile. "Then AI Land was never really about machines."

"Exactly," she replies. "It's about the people who build, teach, and trust them."

And as the car rolls forward into the real world,

you realize — the future of intelligence isn't artificial. It's shared.

Responsibility isn't just protection, it's direction. AI learns from us; our and its future depends on what we teach it.

•••

Beyond the Gates

The sky above AI Land glows softly — threads of light connecting every tower, bridge, and plaza you've crossed.

The air hums not with noise, but with understanding. The gates open quietly behind you as the path ahead stretches wide — part data, part dream — leading into the real world beyond these pages.

The lessons you've gathered here aren't meant to stay within these borders.

They're seeds — ready to grow wherever curiosity leads you next.

Out there, AI Land isn't a place to visit; it's a landscape you now walk through every day — in your work, your art, your learning, your conversations.

And each time you ask, explore, or imagine with care, a small spark of AI Land lights up again.

Kishi: "So… this is it? The end of the journey?"

You smile. "Not the end — just the first loop of the learning spiral."

You take a breath and step forward, feeling how intelligence, both human and artificial, connects it all. The horizon glows softly — new stories forming in the distance.

"The gates never close — they just open wider for the curious."

Kishi: "So what do we do now?"

"Keep asking. Keep exploring. The land will grow with you."

A small compass glows in your hand — engraved with one quiet truth:

The future belongs to the curious.

•••

BONUS KNOWLEDGE STOPS

Optional deeper learning, for the Extra-Curious

The Logic Path — Understanding Algorithms

This is where thinking becomes steps.

You've seen how AI learns from examples — but how does it decide what to do next?

The answer lies in **algorithms** — the quiet logic that turns information into action.

An algorithm is just a clear set of steps to solve a problem —

like a recipe or a to-do list for a computer.

Kishi: "So an algorithm is like instructions?"

"Exactly — step by step, no guessing."

When AI trains, it runs these steps in a loop — each time getting a little better, like practicing a sport or hobby.

act → observe → predict → check → adjust → improve

Modern AI doesn't rely on one giant algorithm, but millions of tiny ones working together — learning in harmony until patterns become second nature.

The Core Essence

- Input → Follow Rules → Check → Adjust → Output

AI doesn't magically "know" — i**t improves by following logic again and again.**

That's the quiet heartbeat of machine intelligence.

•••

Deep Learning — Layers of Understanding

Where small details grow into big meaning

AI doesn't understand the world all at once — it learns step by step, discovering a little more at each stage.

This layered way of learning is called **Deep Learning,** and it's inspired (loosely) by how the human brain learns from experience.

What Deep Learning Really Is

Deep Learning is a method of teaching AI using **neural networks** — digital "webs of tiny learners" that work together to spot patterns across many examples.

Each tiny part learns a small clue, and together they make sense of something big — just like many brain cells working together.

When a neural network has **many layers,** each layer learning something new, we call it **deep** learning.

Kishi: "So 'deep' just means more layers of learning stacked together?"

You: "Exactly — deeper layers, deeper understanding."

How It Learns in Layers

Imagine a group of helpers sitting in a line, each adding a bit more meaning than the one before.

For an image, it might work like this:

- First, notice tiny details like colours and edges.
- Then, group them into simple shapes

- Then, recognize parts like eyes, wheels, or leaves
- Later, understand full objects like a face, a bicycle, or a tree
- Finally, grasp the meaning — a smiling child riding a bicycle under a tree

Tiny clues → shapes → parts → objects → meaning

Each layer passes its discovery forward — and together, they turn raw data into understanding.

Why and How Deep Learning Changed Everything

Before Deep Learning, computers needed humans to write strict rules for everything: "If you see this, then do that."

Deep Learning changed the game because it **learns those rules by itself** from millions of examples — including patterns humans wouldn't notice or know how to explain.

This breakthrough was only possible when two things arrived together:

- Huge amounts of data to learn from
- Extremely powerful computers to process billions of tiny calculations quickly

When data and computing power became available, Deep Learning unlocked a new level of intelligence — one that felt almost intuitive.

<u>**It now powers:**</u>

- language understanding and translation
- image recognition and medical image analysis
- voice assistants that understand tone and intent
- creative tools that write, paint, or compose music

It didn't just improve AI — it transformed what we believed machines could learn.

Two Simple Scenes — Same Idea Behind It

Imagine your tablet trying to learn what a cat looks like.

- At first, every drawing looks like a mystery creature.
- But as it sees more and more cats — fluffy, tiny, black, ginger, sleepy — it starts to notice: pointy ears, whiskers, tails, cat-like faces.
- Soon, it recognises a cat instantly, even if you draw it with sunglasses!

Now imagine learning music styles.

- At first, all songs sound similar.
- But over time, you start noticing layers — beat, instruments, rhythm, voice style — until you instantly know, "That's jazz," or "This sounds like a 90s pop song."

Deep Learning works the same way — layer by layer, pattern by pattern, meaning becomes clear.

A Tiny Peek Behind the Curtain (Only if you're curious)

Here are three simple terms you may hear:

- **Neural Network** → a digital brain made of tiny "neuron-like" units that learn from examples
- **CNN (Convolutional Neural Network)** → excels at understanding images
- **RNN (Recurrent Neural Network)** → designed for sequences like text or speech (later evolved into Transformers)

Different networks specialize in different kinds of understanding — just like different experts in a team.

The Core Essence

Deep Learning learns layer by layer, each step adding richer understanding until patterns become meaning.

It doesn't memorise, it **discovers.** That discovery is what helps machines recognise, understand, and create.

•••

Diffusion Models — Pictures from Pixels

Where chaos turns into creation

Imagine beginning with pure static — like a snowy TV screen.

A diffusion model learns how to turn that noisy chaos into a meaningful picture.

During training, the model is shown millions of real images — and noise is added on purpose.

It practices undoing that noise step by step, learning how to restore structure from randomness.

Now, when you give a prompt like: "A cat wearing sunglasses on a beach", your words act as a target or compass.

At each tiny step, the model asks itself: "Am I closer to the picture they imagined?"

Noise (slowly becomes) → shapes → textures → details → the final image.

Kishi: "So it's like polishing a blurry picture until it becomes clear?"

"Exactly — revealing imagination one tiny improvement at a time."

Because of this gradual, careful process, diffusion models create incredibly rich and realistic visuals — powering tools like DALL·E, Midjourney, and Firefly.

They don't copy — they design from noise, turning imagination into imagery and clarity — pixel by pixel

•••

The Family Tree of Generative Models

Where Diffusion Models find their creative cousins

While models like CNNs and RNNs help AI understand the world, spotting patterns in images, words, and sounds:

Generative Models go a step further — they use what's been learned to create something new.

Generative AI isn't one single invention.

It's a family of different techniques — each imagining in its own way.

Some rebuild, some dream, some compete, and some sculpt clarity from chaos.

At the root of all of them lies data, the foundation of every creative spark.

From there, the family branches outward:

Autoencoders — The Rebuilders

They learn how to compress information and then rebuild it again,

like summarizing a story and retelling it in your own words.

They're great for removing noise, restoring photos, and improving image quality.

VAEs (Variational Autoencoders) — The Dreamers

VAEs learn the essence of data, not exact copies.

They can imagine infinite variations of one thing — like sketching a thousand slightly different sunsets from memory.

GANs (Generative Adversarial Networks) — The Challengers

Two models play a creative game:

one (Generator) tries to create something real; the other (Discriminator) tries to catch the fake.

Through constant competition, both improve until the results are nearly perfect.

This technique powers realistic portraits, artwork, and even fashion or product design.

Diffusion Models — The Artists of Order

In this creative family, they're the patient artists - a framework to turn pixels into imagination, static into structure.

They are the creators who begin with noise and patiently shape meaning.

You have encountered this on the earlier pages.

Kishi peers at the diagram on your tablet.

"So, they all imagine differently — but they share the same roots?"

"Exactly," you reply. "Different minds, same mission — to create from what they've learned."

Generative AI isn't one model but a collection of creative systems, each with its own rhythm for learning, dreaming, and inventing.

Together, they form the art studio of modern machine imagination.

•••

IoT + AI — When Intelligence Steps into the Real World

More and more devices are now smart — connected, sensing, and learning. Your home lights. Your watch. Your car. Even your appliances.

This growing network is called IoT — the Internet of Things

("things" : devices that can talk to each other).

But when AI joins IoT, something bigger happens — devices stop just collecting information; they start understanding and acting on it.

With billions of devices generating massive amounts of data every second,

— humans can't process it all.

AI steps in — quickly finding patterns and making helpful decisions in real time.

- A smartwatch doesn't simply count steps — it learns your heart patterns and suggests healthier habits.
- A smart fridge doesn't just keep things cold — it tracks what's inside and reminds you before food expires.

Sensors + AI → Smart actions: intelligence woven quietly into normal life

- Cars predict when maintenance is needed.
- Farms water crops only when the soil is thirsty.
- Factories prevent accidents before they happen.

AI doesn't only live in screens — it moves into the daily world, making life smoother, safer, and kinder.

In many cases (like in a smart car), AI needs to make instant decisions — right on the device itself, without needing human effort every time

The world becomes one big team, everything helping everything else — where everyday objects start to think and act.

The Core Essence

- Sense → Understand → Decide → Act → Improve: real action powered by digital intelligence.

•••

RAG — When AI Knows when to Look Things Up

Where knowledge stays fresh, accurate, and grounded in facts

AI is great at writing, explaining, and creating — but there's one catch:

sometimes it sounds confident even when it's wrong.

That's because a basic AI model relies only on what it learned during training, which may be outdated, incomplete, or simply missing information.

This is where RAG steps in — Retrieval-Augmented Generation. It helps AI stay accurate by combining two strengths: knowing and checking.

With RAG, the AI doesn't "guess" — it searches for real information first, then uses its language skills to explain the answer clearly.

Part	Role
Retrieval	Finds facts from trusted sources
Augmentation	Adds the right context to enrich the answer
Generation	Explains in clear, human-friendly language

RAG blends three powers into one response:

It's like giving AI both a brain and a library card — so answers stay smart and reliable.

Kishi: "So it's like checking your notes before answering in class?"

You: "Exactly — real smartness is knowing when to look things up."

Why RAG Matters

RAG changes the way AI responds.

Instead of inventing answers, it **verifies, confirms**, and **grounds** them in truth.

It keeps AI practical, helpful, and current.

This is especially valuable when:

- The answer changes often (scores, prices, news)
- Information must be correct (medical, legal, academic)
- The content belongs to you, not the internet (business knowledge)

RAG allows AI to look into specific, approved sources — such as your company documents, knowledge bases, research, manuals, or notes — making it trustworthy for real-world use.

Everyday Examples

Without RAG:

Ask: "Who won yesterday's cricket match?"

→ The model may guess based on old patterns.

With RAG:

Ask: "Who won yesterday's cricket match?"

→ It searches live sources → reads the result → replies accurately.

It's not just for news — it supports day-to-day life too:

- For students: fetches updated definitions, facts, and references
- For families: pulls real recipes, schedules, routes, or reminders
- For travellers: compares current prices, hotels, and weather

In the Real World

RAG is already powering many tools people use daily:

- News and research assistants that cite sources
- Customer support chat that checks real policies before replying
- Business dashboards that read live data, not outdated reports
- Personal knowledge assistants that search your files before answering

RAG doesn't just improve accuracy — **it builds trust.**

The Core Essence

- Ask → Retrieve → Read → Understand → Respond

The AI finds facts first, then uses its intelligence to explain them clearly.

The best AI isn't the one that knows everything; it's the one that knows when to check.

•••

MCP - The Language That Lets AI Use Tools in the Real World

Where AI learns what's available and possible — safely and smoothly

AI can think, learn, and create... but for a long time, it struggled with something very human: **doing things in the real world.**

This was not because it lacked intelligence — but because tools and systems around it didn't speak a common language. Different apps, websites, databases, and devices each had its own "way of talking."

If you wanted an AI to use a new tool, developers had to manually wire the connection.

Every new feature needed fresh code, testing, and maintenance. It worked — but it was fragile, time-consuming, and limited.

Kishi: "So AI had the brains... but every tool spoke a different language?"

"Exactly. Everyone was smart — but no one understood each other."

That's where **MCP** comes in — the Model Context Protocol. It gives AI and tools a shared way to communicate, collaborate, and act with clarity.

Why MCP Matters

Before MCP, connecting AI to tools felt like building bridges one brick at a time.

Each tool needed custom code to explain:

- what it could do
- what information it needed
- and how to ask it to do something

With MCP, tools can publish their abilities in a common, simple format.

Think of MCP like a global directory and instruction guide that tools share.

It tells an AI:

- "Here's what I can do,"
- "Here's how to talk to me,"
- "Here are the rules for using me."

Instead of guessing or relying on pre-wired setups, AI can now **discover** and **work with tools more independently and safely.**

Kishi: "So MCP doesn't give tools power — it helps them share their powers?"

"You got it. It's not the magic — it's the map."

Before vs After MCP

Before MCP	With MCP
Each tool needed custom code to connect	Tools describe themselves once, in a standard way
AI could only use tools it was pre-programmed to use	AI can discover available tools and understand how to use them
Fragile, one-by-one integrations	Flexible, reusable, easier to maintain
Tools struggled to work together	Multiple tools can coordinate smoothly
Unclear access and permissions	Clear rules and safe boundaries

MCP doesn't make AI "take over" — it brings clarity, safety, and confidence to how AI uses tools.

How MCP Works

1. **Tools share their abilities**

, like posting a menu: "Here's what I can do, and here's how to ask."

2. **AI understands the instructions**

It uses a shared format called a schema — like an instant instruction manual.

3. **Use happens with permissions**

You stay in control of what the AI can and cannot access.

4. Smooth teamwork

Tools and AI (and sometimes other agents) can now work together as a team.

Kishi: "So it's like devices finally using the same charger?"

"Sort of — one standard makes everyone compatible."

A School Project Example

Imagine a student is preparing a school project on "Rainforests."

With MCP-style teamwork:

- A research tool finds kid-friendly facts
- An image tool collects rainforest photos you may use
- A calendar tool helps plan your submission timeline
- A writing assistant helps outline your project

The AI isn't doing your homework — it's gathering resources and helping you stay organized.

A Home Life Example — "Smooth Sunday Reset"

You tell your AI: "Help me reset the home for the week."

With MCP, the AI could coordinate:

- A checklist tool to list weekly chores
- A grocery tool to see what's running low
- A calendar tool to find time for laundry and cooking
- A music tool to set a mood for the day
- A budget tool to suggest weekly savings

Because these tools speak MCP, the AI can understand, sequence, and guide them — without new code for each one.

Why MCP Is Safe

MCP keeps the user in control.

- You decide what the AI can connect to.
- Tools clearly define what actions are allowed.
- Logs record what happened and why
- Boundaries are built in

MCP isn't about letting AI do "everything" — it's about enabling AI to plan, discover, and do **the right things, clearly and safely.**

The Core Essence

- Tools publish what they can do → AI discovers the right tool →

Rules control access → Smooth, safe cooperation

•••

The Math Behind Intelligence

How numbers quietly power smart machines

AI might seem like pure imagination — a world of stories, images, and conversations.

But underneath it all lies something quieter, older, and deeply human — mathematics.

Every time an AI recognizes a pattern, predicts a word, or paints a picture, it's using math to see structure where we see chaos.

Math isn't just the backbone of AI — it's the rhythm that helps it learn, reason, and improve.

Why Math Matters

When we teach AI, we're really teaching it to measure change, compare possibilities, and choose what fits best — exactly what math has always done.

Here's how different kinds of math quietly guide AI through its learning journey.

Statistics — Finding patterns in the noise

Statistics helps AI separate signal from clutter.

It looks across millions of examples and asks, "What usually happens?"

That's how an AI can tell if a photo looks more like a cat than a cloud — it learns what's normal, what's rare, and what's surprising.

It's the math of **trends, averages, and confidence.**

Linear Algebra — Turning the world into numbers

For AI to "see" or "read," everything — text, sound, or image — must first become numbers.

Linear Algebra provides that crucial translation.

It organizes all this information into vectors and matrices so AI can efficiently recognize shapes, meanings, and relationships.

When an image generator creates art or a chatbot understands tone, Linear Algebra is the invisible map connecting ideas inside the model.

Calculus — Learning through tiny changes

Calculus helps AI adjust itself, step by step, until it performs better.

When a model makes an error, calculus tells it precisely:

how much and in which direction to adjust its internal settings.

This process — called optimization — is how AI slowly learns to make smarter predictions.

It's like steering a ship toward a lighthouse: each small correction brings it closer to the right path.

Probability — Thinking in "maybe" instead of "must"

AI doesn't always know the answer — it guesses intelligently.

Probability helps it weigh options when things are uncertain, quantifying how likely each outcome is.

That's how an AI predicts your next word in a sentence, estimates which movie you might like, or detects spam.

It's the math of uncertainty, helping machines act confidently even when the world is fuzzy.

•••

THE TOOLS INDEX

Your compass to the world of AI tools and possibilities

Scan the QR code to explore the Tools Index online — all categories, AI tools list, and clickable links in one place.

LIST OF AI TOOLS

Design & Visual Creation

Tool	What it Does	Website/Link
DAAL-E	Creates images from text descriptions.	openai.com/dall-e
Midjourney	Generates artistic, high-quality visuals.	midjourney.com
Leonardo AI	Concept art and game visualization.	leonardo.ai
Canva Magic Studio	AI design for layouts and presentations.	canva.com
Adobe Firefly	Image generation within Creative Cloud.	adobe.com/firefly

Writing & Communication

Tool	What It Does	Website / Link
ChatGPT	Conversational assistant for writing and ideas.	chat.openai.com
Claude	Long-context reasoning and document analysis.	claude.ai
Gemini	Gemini Google's AI for writing and data tasks.	gemini.google.com
Jasper	Generates marketing and advertising copy.	jasper.ai
Copy.ai	Creates blogs, emails, and product texts.	copy.ai
GrammarlyGO	Suggests rewrites and tone adjustments.	grammarly.com
Wordtune	Refines sentences for clarity and flow.	wordtune.com

Music and Audio

Tool	What It Does	Website / Link
Suno	Generates complete songs from text prompts.	suno.ai
Udio	Composes music by mood and genre.	udio.com
AIVA	Creates cinematic and classical music.	aiva.ai
Mubert	Produces copyright-safe background music.	mubert.com
ElevenLabs	Generates realistic voiceovers and speech.	elevenlabs.io
Play.ht	Converts text into audio narration.	play.ht

Video and Animation

Tool	What It Does	Website / Link
Runway ML	Generates and edits AI videos.	runwayml.com
Pika Labs	Creates videos from text or storyboards.	pika.art
Kaiber	Animates still images into motion.	kaiber.ai
Synthesia	Talking avatars for education and training.	synthesia.io
HeyGen	Custom avatars and video presenters.	heygen.com
Nano Banana	On-device AI for image and video creation.	aistudio.google.com

Coding and Development

Tool	What it Does	Website/Link
GitHub Copilot	Suggests code while you type.	github.com/ features/copilot
Replit Ghostwrit- er	In-IDE AI coding assistant.	replit.com
replit.com	AI-first code editor and explainer.	cursor.so
Gemini Code Assist	Google's coding helper for Cloud tools.	cloud.google. com/ gemini- code-assist
Claude	Code reasoning and debugging support.	claude.ai

Productivity and Business

Tool	What it Does	Website/Link
Microsoft Copilot	Automates tasks in Office apps.	microsoft.com/copilot
Google Duet AI	AI in Docs, Sheets, and Slides.	workspace.google.com/duet-ai
Notion AI	Summarizes notes and plans tasks.	notion.so
ChatGPT Teams	Secure collaboration with AI chat.	openai.com
Gemini Workspace	Integrates AI across Gmail and Docs.	gemini.google.com

Video and Animation

Tool	What It Does	Website / Link
Khanmigo	AI tutor by Khan Academy.	khanacademy.org
Quizlet Q-Chat	Practice and quiz AI companion.	quizlet.com
Socratic	Homework help with step-by-step guidance.	socratic.org
Perplexity AI	Conversational research assistant.	perplexity.ai
Gemini Education	Personalized teaching and class content.	gemini.google.com
ChatGPT Edu	Academic use for learning and feedback.	openai.com/edu

Health and Wellness

Tool	What It Does	Website / Link
Ada Health	Symptom checker and insights.	ada.com
Noom	AI-driven behavior change and personalized nutrition coaching.	noom.com
Fitbit AI Insights	Analyzes fitness and recovery data.	fitbit.com
WHOOP Coach	Suggests training based on metrics.	whoop.com
Woebot	Mental-health chat support.	woebothealth.com
Wysa	Emotional wellness assistant.	wysa.io

Entertainment and Storytelling

Tool	What It Does	Website / Link
Inworld AI	Builds interactive game characters.	inworld.ai
NovelAI	Generates fiction and scenes for writers.	novelai.net
Sudowrite	Assists authors with editing and inspiration.	sudowrite.com
Gemini Advanced	Long-form reasoning and creative ideation.	gemini.google.com

Autonomous Agents & Frameworks

Tool	What It Does	Website / Link
AutoGPT	Open-source agent that can plan and execute multi-steWWp goals using GPT models.	github.com/Torantulino/Auto-GPT
Devin AI	Autonomous "software engineer" that codes, tests, and deploys projects independently.	cognition-labs.com
n8n (AI Agents)	No-code automation platform where AI and apps connect through workflows and MCP-based agents.	n8n.io
CrewAI	Framework for managing multiple collaborating AI agents that divide and complete tasks together.	crewai.com
LangChain Agents	Toolset that allows language models to reason, access APIs, and use real-world tools safely.	langchain.com
LlamaIndex	Framework that lets AI retrieve and use external data intelligently — foundation for retrieval-augmented agents.	llamaindex.ai

Cursor AI	Smart coding assistant that writes, edits, and refactors code contextually — a developer's co-pilot.	cursor.sh
Model Context Protocol (MCP)	Open standard that allows AI tools and agents to discover, connect, and collaborate securely.	modelcontextprotocol.io
Adept ACT-1	Experimental agent that performs software actions directly through natural language commands.	adept.ai
SuperAGI	Developer framework for building and deploying fully autonomous, goal-driven AI agents.	superagi.com

GLOSSARY OF FRIENDLY AI TERMS

A simple reference for curious minds

A – C

AI (Artificial Intelligence) — A computer system designed to learn, decide, and solve problems — possessing human-like abilities without being human. (→ The Welcome Gate)

Agentic AI — AI that doesn't just respond — it plans, acts, and adapts on behalf of a user. (→ Agents Avenue)

AI Agent — A specialized digital helper that performs focused tasks like searching, summarizing, or organizing — often working under an Agentic AI system. (→ Agents Avenue)

Algorithm — A clear set of steps that tells a computer exactly what to do — like a recipe for solving a problem. (→ Bonus Stop — Algorithms)

Autonomy (in AI) — The level of independence an AI system has to make decisions or act without constant human guidance. (→ Agents Avenue)

Bias (in AI) — When AI gives unfair or skewed results

because the data it learned from was not balanced or diverse. (→ The Data Tower)

Chatbot — A conversational program that interacts with people using text or voice — like ChatGPT or a voice assistant. (→ The Prompt Plaza)

Compute Power — The processing 'strength' of a system — how fast it can learn, generate, or reason. (→ The Learning Bridge)

Context Window — The amount of information an AI model can read, remember, and consider at once before replying. (→ LLM Library)

Creativity (in AI) — The ability of AI to generate new ideas, art, or writing based on learned patterns — not imagination, but intelligent generation. (→ The Creativity Corner)

D – F

Data — Information that AI learns from — text, numbers, images, or sounds. (→ The Data Tower)

Dataset — A structured collection of data used to train or test AI models. (→ The Data Tower)

Deep Learning — A form of machine learning that teaches AI to learn in many layers — each layer recognizing more complex patterns. (→ The Learning Bridge)

Diffusion Model — An AI system that turns random digital 'noise' into detailed images — like sculpting clarity from chaos. (→ Bonus Stop — Diffusion Models)

Embedding — A way to represent words, images, or sounds as numbers so AI can understand relationships between them. (→ LLM Library)

Ethical AI — AI designed and used with fairness, transparency, and accountability in mind. (→ Beyond the Gates — Responsible AI)

Fairness — Ensuring AI performs equally well for everyone — avoiding bias or discrimination. (→ Beyond the Gates — Responsible AI)

Fine-Tuning — Teaching an existing AI model new, focused examples so it becomes better at specific tasks. (→ The Model Museum)

Feedback Loop — A process where AI improves by learning from the results of its own actions and user responses. (→ The Learning Bridge)

G – L

Generative AI — AI that creates — text, art, music, or video — from patterns it has learned. (→ The Creativity Corner)

Grounding (in AI) — Tying AI's responses to real-world facts and verified data — keeping creativity rooted in truth. (→ Beyond the Gates — Responsible AI)

Hallucination (in AI) — When AI confidently gives an answer that sounds right… but isn't true. (→ LLM Library)

Inference — When a trained model uses what it already knows to predict or respond — applying learning in real time. (→ The Learning Bridge)

IoT (Internet of Things) — Everyday connected devices — watches, cars, lights — sharing and learning from data. (→ Bonus Stop — IoT + AI)

Large Language Model (LLM) — An AI trained on massive amounts of text that reads, writes, and reasons in natural language. (→ LLM Library)

Latency — The delay between giving AI a task and getting a response — lower latency means faster results. (→ Tool Market)

Learning (in AI) — How AI improves over time — finding patterns, adjusting parameters, and refining predictions. (→ The Learning Bridge)

LLM Guardrails — Safety filters that help large language models avoid harmful, biased, or unsafe outputs. (→ Beyond the Gates — Responsible AI)

M – O

Machine Learning (ML) — When computers learn from examples instead of following explicit instructions. (→ The Learning Bridge)

Memory (in AI) — What AI retains from past interactions to maintain context or continuity. (→ Agents Avenue)

Model — The 'brain' of AI — built from data and algorithms that can make predictions, generate, or classify. (→ The Model Museum)

Multimodal AI — AI that can understand and combine text, images, sound, and other types of input. (→ The Creativity Corner)

Neural Network — A web of digital 'neurons' inspired by the human brain — the building blocks of deep learning. (→ The Learning Bridge)

Noise (in images) — Random static or fuzz that image models learn to turn into meaningful pictures. (→ Bonus Stop — Diffusion Models)

P – R

Parameters — Tiny adjustable values inside a model that define what it has learned — its internal memory map. (→ The Model Museum)

Personalization — How AI adapts its tone, suggestions, or responses to fit an individual's style and preferences. (→ Tool Market)

Prompt — Your instruction or question to an AI — what you type or say to get a response. (→ The Prompt Plaza)

Prompt Engineering — Designing clear, thoughtful prompts to guide AI toward the best results. (→ The Prompt Plaza)

Reinforcement Learning — A training method where AI learns through trial, feedback, and rewards — like learning by doing. (→ The Learning Bridge)

RAG (Retrieval-Augmented Generation) — An AI approach that looks up real information before answering — combining search and generation. (→ Bonus Stop — RAG)

Reasoning (in AI) — The ability to connect ideas and make step-by-step logical conclusions — not just predict the next word. (→ Agents Avenue)

Responsible AI — Developing and using AI that respects human values, fairness, and safety — balancing innovation with ethics. (→ Beyond the Gates — Responsible AI)

S – T

Safety Layers (in AI) — Multiple safeguards built into AI systems to prevent harmful, biased, or misleading content. (→ Beyond the Gates — Responsible AI)

Small Language Model (SLM) — A compact, efficient cousin of LLMs — designed for faster, private, and device-friendly use. (→ LLM Library)

Tokens — Tiny text units — often parts of words — that AI reads and predicts to form sentences. (→ LLM Library)

Training — The process of feeding data into a model so it learns patterns and relationships. (→ The Learning Bridge)

Transformer — A neural architecture that helps AI understand meaning and relationships across long texts. (→ LLM Library)

Transparency (in AI) — Making AI systems and their decision-making clear and understandable for users. (→ Beyond the Gates — Responsible AI)

U – Z

Use Case — A real-world scenario where AI is applied to solve a problem or add value. (→ Tool Market)

Vision Model — AI that can 'see' — recognizing or generating images and videos. (→ The Creativity Corner)

Weights — The numbers that store what an AI model has learned; adjusted during training to improve performance. (→ The Model Museum)

THANK YOU NOTE FROM THE AUTHOR

Thank you for reading.

Whether this was your first step into Artificial Intelligence or one stop along a longer exploration, I hope the stories, examples, and analogies made the concepts feel clear, friendly, and meaningful.

If this book helped you understand AI a little better — even in a small way — that means a lot.

Your feedback matters.

Even a short review or a single line helps other readers discover the book and gives me guidance for what comes next.

If you enjoyed the book, **please leave a review on the platform where you purchased it.**

If you found it helpful, please share it with a friend, colleague, student, or curious mind who may benefit from it.

Thank you again — for reading, for exploring, and for stepping into this world with curiosity.

— Nitin

CREDITS & ACKNOWLEDGMENTS

This book was created with curiosity, persistence, and a desire to make learning approachable and enjoyable.

My heartfelt thanks to everyone who supported this journey — family, friends, early readers, and the many conversations that shaped and refined ideas along the way.

This book was shaped through research, lived experience, and AI-assisted tools, including ChatGPT, Gemini, Copilot for drafting and enhancements. All decisions, direction, and final editing were made by the author.

A special appreciation to global open-source and AI communities whose work continues to expand access, accelerate learning, and inspire new possibilities.